D0579001

Take 3 Cooks

Take 3 Cooks

NANETTE NEWMAN

and her daughters EMMA FORBES and SARAH STANDING

HarperCollins*Publishers*

To the three greatest non-cooks we've ever had the pleasure of cooking for,
Bryan, John and Graham.

First published in 1996 by HarperCollins*Publishers* London
Reprinted 1996

Some of the recipes have been published previously in *Entertaining with Nanette Newman* and in titles by Nanette Newman and Emma Forbes.

Text © Nanette Newman, Emma Forbes, Sarah Standing 1996

All rights reserved

The authors assert the moral right to be identified as authors of this work

FOOD PHOTOGRAPHER: *Roger Stowell*
STYLIST: *Penny Markham*
HOME ECONOMIST: *Gillian MacLaurin*
COVER PHOTOGRAPHER: *Harry Ormisher*
COVER MAKE-UP AND HAIR: *Michaeljohn*
INDEXER: *Susan Bosanko*

For HarperCollins*Publishers*:

COMMISSIONING EDITOR: *Barbara Dixon*
EDITOR: *Becky Humphreys*
DESIGNER: *Graeme Andrew*

A catalogue record for this book is available from the British Library
ISBN 000 412994 6

Typeset in Goudy
Colour reproductions by Colourscan, Singapore
Printed and bound by Rotolito Lombarda, Milan, Italy

BACK COVER PHOTOGRAPHS: (*clockwise from left to right*)
Soured Cream Pound Cake, Citrus Cake, Pistachio Cookies; Seafood Supper;
Oreo Cookie Cheesecake; Gingered Salmon en Croûte

CONTENTS

USEFUL FACTS AND FIGURES

These are just some useful points that we thought you might need:

METRICATION

Throughout this book we have given quantities in both metric and Imperial measures – we hope this makes the transition to metric a little gentler. Since exact conversion from Imperial to metric does not usually give practical working quantities, the metric measures have been rounded to the nearest unit of 25 grams.

The table below gives the recommended equivalents. However, remember that when making any of the recipes in this book, follow only one set of measures as they are not interchangeable.

GRAMS	OUNCES
25	1
50	2
75	3
100	4
150	5
175	6
200	7
225	8
250	9
275	10
300	11
350	12
375	13
400	14
425	15
450	16 (1 lb)

LIQUID MEASURES

The millilitre has been used in this book and the following table gives a few examples:

PINTS	MILLILITRES	AMERICAN CUPS
¼	150	⅔
½	300	1¼
¾	450	scant 2 cups
1	600	2½

SPOON MEASURES

Spoon measures are level unless otherwise stated.

EGGS

All eggs used refer to size 3 unless otherwise stated. When large eggs are used this refers to sizes 1 or 2. Please be aware that current Government health guidelines recommend not eating recipes containing uncooked eggs if pregnant or elderly.

QUANTITIES

We have suggested how many people each recipe will serve, but naturally, it depends upon your own assessment of your friends' appetites.

SEASONINGS

Throughout the book we have mainly used fresh herbs but should you use dried, then just remember to halve the quantities.

We are all health-conscious today and many of us wish to cut down on salt, therefore we have not given salt and pepper quantities – this is best left to your own taste and conscience.

STOCKS

There is no doubt that home-made stock is by far the best, but don't go into intensive care if you have to use a stock cube. We all do it occasionally.

FATS

Should you prefer to substitute margarine for butter in the recipes they will still work.

OVEN TEMPERATURES

Here are the recommended equivalents:

	C	F	GAS MARK
Very cool	110	225	¼
	120	250	½
Cool	140	275	1
	150	300	2
Moderate	160	325	3
	180	350	4
Moderately hot	190	375	5
	200	400	6
Hot	220	425	7
	230	450	8
Very hot	240	475	9

Foreword by Nanette

I think I've been lucky to have daughters who, right from the word go, were interested in cooking. I didn't learn to cook until I was married, and I'm amazed my marriage survived some of my (literally) burnt offerings. I am living proof that the way to a man's heart is not necessarily through his stomach. Unlike their mother, when Sarah and Emma got married they were both marvellous cooks.

We have all three developed different styles and tastes along the way – but certain things we have in common. We all hate endless hours spent in the kitchen, we like entertaining family and friends at home, we love collecting recipes and hate pretentious food (the sort of meals that are so complex and over-sauced that you can hardly recognise what you are eating).

I think that when certain foods are in season and at their peak, the less done to them the better. A superb fish simply grilled and served with large chunks of lemon, vegetables when young and tender, speak for themselves and should not be messed around. A perfect, ripe pear with some cheese and home-made ginger biscuits – delicious! And...well, you know what I mean.

However, part of the fun of cooking is knowing when to leave well alone, or when a little invention is necessary. We all seem to lead chaotic lives, juggling the hours in the day so that everything gets done, and the three of us agree that, when you have time, cooking for everyone is a pleasure. But there are times when all you want to muster is Marmite on toast. We often take short cuts and indulge in some clever cheating because it often saves your sanity. We'd rather have a scrambled egg and a bit of a laugh with a friend than some elaborate meal where the hostess is too exhausted and demented to enjoy it.

So, there it is – we've put together the recipes we've tried and liked, been given by friends or developed in some way ourselves and which we enjoy making.

We hope looking through the book will give you a few ideas for one of those days when the kids are hell, the ironing has piled up, you were at a party the night before, the weather has turned nasty and you need a bit of help. This book, taken with a cup of coffee, might well do the trick.

Foreword by Sarah

I think I must have always been interested in cooking because it's something I've always been aware of doing. From my earliest efforts of mud-pies to truly disgusting Ribena milkshakes, I was always encouraged by my mother to experiment in the kitchen.

When I left home at seventeen I used to have flamboyantly ambitious dinner parties, and never seemed to lose my nerve, regardless of who was coming or what was cooking. I would attempt soufflés for 20 people – the act of a madwoman – yet I presented them with gusto and a grin, kept the plonk and the conversation flowing and somehow managed to pull it off.

I was lucky enough to marry a man whose concept of a full fridge was one stacked with two eggs, a pint of milk and a dead tomato and whose idea of cooking was switching the toaster on, so I quickly realised I was batting on an easy wicket and that anything I produced in the kitchen was greeted with gratitude and wonder. I've now got three children, so my main criteria for entertaining is minimum effort with maximum results.

I write while the children are at school, clock off for the day when they come home and then spend an awful lot of time getting homework wrong. By the time I've read Noddy my brain is addled. I don't have the time nor the inclination to spend hours messing around with fiddly recipes. I love having friends over to dinner, and I want to be able to enjoy the evening as much as they do.

I've found that one has to realise one's limitations. If you use fabulously fresh ingredients, try to veer towards simple dishes that don't take days to prepare, cut down on anything that's complicated and have a larder stocked with enough basics to survive a famine – it is possible to have a life after the maths homework is cleared away.

Being married to an actor, I often think having a dinner party is not dissimilar to the curtain going up on a play. As long as the set looks good, you're surrounded by a great cast and you know your lines, it'll be alright on the night.

Foreword by Emma

Cooking has always been something I've enjoyed. I love trying out new recipes and experimenting. I was encouraged to do this as a child (sometimes with horrendous results!). When I was about eight years old I remember someone saying, "Presentation is everything when it comes to serving food", so when my mother next had a dinner party, I offered to make the pudding, putting my heart and soul into the decoration of it. I walked into the dining room triumphantly bearing my exotic, over-the-top offering and announced, with great modesty, "This is the best pudding you've ever had." Whereupon, I tripped and my creation flew across the room and landed on a guest's lap. I was, of course, inconsolable. (I don't think the woman the pudding landed on was too thrilled either.) It taught me that, yes, presentation is important, but not the most important thing, and that also it's safer to wait for praise after your efforts have been tried. Still, I was only eight. However it didn't deter me for long, and I'm happy to say I have never had a repeat performance, although come to think of it, during the three years I did a cooking slot on *Going Live!* we did sometimes come pretty near to the odd mishap.

Both Graham, my husband, and I work very long hours, and frequently when I get home from the studio I have to cook quickly with the minimum of fuss, but now I'm used to it. I am very fortunate that I live close to shops that are open day and night so I can always get a missing ingredient or rush to the Italian deli for some superb fresh pasta, a hunk of parmesan and flowers from round the corner for the table.

My husband can't cook a thing, but is a joy to cook for. He loves eating, will try anything, and is particularly into what he calls 'light puddings' – i.e. anything loaded with cream and chocolate (the mere mention of tiramisu makes his evening). He is also brilliant at being appreciative – so important when you're the cook.

I suppose my method of cooking is governed by my life style – informal because I have an open-plan kitchen and dining room where space has to be cleverly worked out. So these recipes I've included in our collection are those that I've tried and tested many times and that have been given the seal of approval by those I've cooked for.

BEGINNING THE DAY

Some people couldn't possibly begin the day without breakfast. Others, like me, can only just stagger around, clutching a cup of coffee. That is, until I'm away from home. As soon as I go abroad I become a breakfast addict.

Once when we were living in France, shooting a film, I ate freshly baked croissants, white peaches and *café au lait* every day – perfection! When we are in America I can't wait to wake up to crispy bacon, easy-over eggs and hash brown potatoes – and I've even succumbed to the odd waffle topped with melted butter and maple syrup. However, as soon as I return home, it all becomes a calorie-ridden dream.

I do like getting breakfast for others, on the assumption that, like me, friends staying in my house are 'away-breakfast-eaters'.

The following recipes are breakfast and brunch ideas that are equally good, in some cases, for starters or late-night snacks. Whenever you choose to make them, they are lovely ways of spoiling friends and family.

Nanette

HONEYED TOAST

Serves 2

2 thick slices granary bread,
toasted
2 teaspoons honey
1 banana, thinly sliced
½ mango, peeled, stoned and
thinly sliced
2 teaspoons Demerara sugar

Staying with a friend in Barbados I was given this for breakfast one day. I liked it so much that I had it every morning for the entire holiday.

Spread the toasted granary bread with the honey. Top with the sliced banana and mango. Sprinkle evenly with the Demerara sugar and cook under a preheated, very hot grill until golden and bubbly, about ½ minute.
Serve while still hot.

PEANUT BUTTER FRENCH TOAST

Serves 2

4 slices wholewheat or
raisin bread
2 tablespoons chunky
peanut butter
1 egg
¼ teaspoon salt
4 tablespoons milk
25 g (1 oz) butter

I invented this recipe for my daughter India when she was three because she loved peanut butter, yet hated breakfast. If eaten with some sliced fresh fruit, it's actually a great nutritional start to the day.

Use the bread and peanut butter to make two sandwiches. Beat the egg with the salt and milk, mixing well. Dip the sandwiches into the egg mixture to coat on all sides.
Melt the butter in a frying pan, add the sandwiches and sauté until golden – about 2 minutes on each side. Drain on absorbent paper.
Serve while still warm cut into thick fingers.

* Incidentally, this recipe is only for people who weigh less than 25 lb or who won't mind putting on 25 lb before the newspaper arrives!

BREAKFAST APPLES

Baked apples are generally served as a dessert but they are just wonderful for breakfast served with Greek yoghurt.

Serves 4

4 large cooking apples, cored
75 g (3 oz) dates, dried figs or apricots, chopped
4 teaspoons honey

150 ml (¼ pint) apple juice
25 g (1 oz) butter

Make a shallow cut around the waist of each apple to prevent the skins from bursting during cooking. Fill the cavities of the apples with chopped dates or figs, pressing the filling down firmly. Place in an ovenproof dish which is just large enough to hold the apples snugly. Spoon a teaspoonful of honey over each apple and pour over the apple juice. Dot with the butter.

Bake in a preheated oven, 180°C/350°F (gas mark 4), for about 45 minutes, basting from time to time, until the apples are tender but not fallen – keep an eye on them. Serve warm or cold with Greek or vanilla yoghurt.

EVENING APPLES: Prepare and cook as above but stuff the apples with 25 g (1oz) raisins mixed with 25 g (1oz) soft brown sugar, 1 tablespoon honey, 1 peeled and chopped banana, ½ teaspoon ground cinnamon and 1 tablespoon brandy. Serve warm with whipped cream.

Emma

Breakfast Apples

YOGHURT WITH FRUIT AND HONEY

Serves 4

600 ml (1 pint) Greek yoghurt
2-4 tablespoons clear honey
4 tablespoons muesli
2 tablespoons dried blueberries
2 tablespoons flaked almonds
about 225 g (8 oz) of your
favourite fruit

Mix the yoghurt with the honey, muesli, blueberries and almonds. Spoon into bowls and top with your favourite fruit.

HIGH PROTEIN 'GET-UP-AND-GO' MILKSHAKE

Serves 2

600 ml (1 pint) milk
1 large ripe banana, peeled
1 tablespoon honey
1 teaspoon lecithin granules
(available from health
food shops)
1 egg
1 teaspoon coffee powder

Place the milk, banana, honey, lecithin granules, egg and coffee powder in a blender or food processor and purée until smooth and creamy. Pour into tall glasses.

BREAKFAST BAGELS

Makes 4

4 bagels
8 rashers lean back bacon,
rinded
4 tablespoons cream cheese

Split the bagels in half and toast. Grill the bacon until crisp, drain on absorbent paper. Spread one side of each bagel with the cream cheese. Top with the bacon and sandwich together.

BLTs IN MUFFINS

Makes 8

8 wholemeal English muffins
8 rashers lean back bacon,
rinded
about ¼ shredded Iceberg
lettuce
3 tomatoes, thinly sliced
4 tablespoons mayonnaise

Split the muffins in half and toast. Grill the bacon until crisp, drain on absorbent paper. Sandwich the warm toasted muffins with the lettuce, tomatoes, bacon and mayonnaise.

FIG OMELETTE: Drizzle honey over 2 finely chopped, fresh, ripe figs and leave overnight. Make an omelette in the usual way using 2 eggs beaten with 1 dessertspoon of milk and 1 tablespoon of caster sugar. Cook in butter until set. Spread the chopped figs over half of the omelette and fold to serve.

Nanette

EGG-FILLED TOMATOES

You could try serving these with Sarah's Cheddar Cheese and Basil Popovers (opposite) and a crisp salad for lunch.

Serves 4

4 very large tomatoes
4 rashers streaky bacon, rinded
50 g (2 oz) button mushrooms, wiped and
chopped

15 g (½ oz) butter
4 eggs
salt
freshly ground black pepper

Lightly grease an ovenproof dish. Cut the tops off the tomatoes and carefully scoop out the flesh using a teaspoon. Turn the tomato shells upside-down and leave to drain.

Grill the bacon until crisp, drain on absorbent paper then crumble. Melt the butter in a small pan, add the mushrooms and cook until just tender. Mix half of the

mushrooms with the bacon and spoon into the tomato shells.

Crack an egg carefully into each tomato, season with salt and pepper to taste then top with the remaining bacon. Place the tomatoes in the ovenproof dish and bake in a preheated oven 190°C/375°F (gas mark 5), for about 8 minutes, or until the eggs are cooked to your liking.

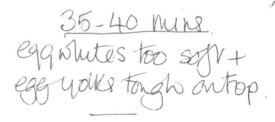

35-40 mins
egg whites too soft +
egg yolks tough on top.

probably needs bacon for good taste — the mushroom/cream option rather bland.

VARIATION: Prepare and cook as above but leave out the bacon. Mix all the mushrooms with 3 tablespoons double cream and spoon into the tomato shells. Crack an egg carefully into each tomato, season with salt and pepper and sprinkle with a little grated cheese. Bake as above.

CHEDDAR CHEESE AND BASIL POPOVERS

I'd never heard of (or tasted) popovers until I went to live in America, and now I'm hooked. These are deliciously light breads that go with everything – fruit salads for breakfast, eggs for brunch or soups and salads for dinner. The basil is optional and can be left out or replaced with your own favourite herb. In America you can buy special popover tins but deep muffin tins work just as well.

Makes 9

2 eggs
300 ml (½ pint) milk
150 g (5 oz) self-raising flour
¼ teaspoon salt

40 g (1½ oz) butter, melted
2-3 tablespoons finely chopped fresh basil
75 g (3 oz) Cheddar cheese, grated

Beat the eggs until foamy then gradually add the milk, mixing well. Sift the flour with the salt and beat into the egg mixture until smooth and creamy. Stir in the melted butter and basil.

Half-fill 9 thickly buttered muffin tins or ramekin dishes with the batter. Top with the grated cheese and the remaining batter. Bake in a preheated oven, 200°C/ 400°F (gas mark 6), for 15 minutes.

Reduce the oven temperature to 180°C/350°F (gas mark 4), and cook for a further 20 minutes, or until well puffed and golden (rather like individual soufflés). Allow to cool slightly before removing from the dishes or tins.

Serve these delicious popovers hot with lashings of butter.

LEMON MARMALADE AND TOAST PUDDING

This is one of those impressive little numbers that you can easily whip up when you have friends for breakfast.

Serves 4-6

40 g (1½ oz) butter
8 large slices bread, crusts removed
4 tablespoons lemon marmalade

600 ml (1 pint) milk
4 eggs, beaten

Butter each slice of bread on both sides and sandwich together in pairs with the lemon marmalade. Cut each sandwich into four triangles.

Place the bread in the base of a greased 1.5-litre (2½-pint) ovenproof dish. Beat the eggs in a bowl. Heat the milk in the pan until very hot but not boiling. Pour the milk over the eggs and whisk until well mixed. Pour over the bread and leave to soak for 10-15 minutes. Bake in a preheated oven, 200°C/400°F (gas mark 6), for 30-40 minutes until golden, well-risen and set.

Serve warm with slices of fresh orange and *crème fraîche* if liked.

To make this a SAVOURY TOAST PUDDING, make the sandwiches using slices of cheese rather than marmalade. Season with salt and pepper and sprinkle the top with grated cheese and chopped parsley before baking.

Nanette

Lemon Marmalade and Toast Pudding

MARMALADE MUFFINS

We used to make muffins when we were children. Although you can buy muffins in any supermarket, you can't beat home-made!

Makes 9

100 g (4 oz) plain wholemeal flour
100 g (4 oz) self-raising flour
1 tablespoon baking powder
25 g (1 oz) sultanas
2 tablespoons soft brown sugar

grated rind of 1 orange
2 eggs, beaten
150 ml (¼ pint) milk
50 ml (2 fl oz) sunflower oil
4 tablespoons orange marmalade

Sift the flours and baking powder together in a large mixing bowl, adding any pieces of bran that remain in the sieve.

Stir in the sultanas, sugar and orange rind. In another bowl beat the eggs with the milk and sunflower oil. Add the egg mixture and stir lightly until just blended. Be careful not to over beat.

Half-fill 9 greased muffin tins with the mixture. Top each with a teaspoon of the marmalade, then spoon the remaining muffin mixture over the top. The muffin tins should be about three-quarters full for baking. Bake in a preheated oven, 200°C/400°F (gas mark 6), for 20-25 minutes. Leave the muffins to cool slightly then turn out and eat while still warm with butter.

These muffins are doubly delicious if served with TANGERINE BUTTER Simply put the juice of 1 tangerine plus the pulp (without seeds) in a blender or food processor with 100 g (4 oz) butter and 2 teaspoons icing sugar. Blend or process until well mixed. Add the finely grated rind of 1 tangerine and whirl again. Put into a small dish, cover and chill for at least 30 minutes.

VARIATIONS: To your basic muffin mixture add 100g (4 oz) of the following in place of the sultanas, orange rind and marmalade: fresh blueberries • hulled blackberries • chopped dates • chopped apricots or peaches • chopped apple with a pinch of ground cinnamon • chopped pear with the grated rind of small orange • half raisins and half chopped nuts • fresh cranberries

PANCAKES

250 ml (8 fl oz) milk
250 ml (8 fl oz) water
4 large eggs
½ teaspoon salt
1 tablespoon sugar
4 tablespoons melted butter
225 g (8 oz) flour

Makes about 16 pancakes

I am crazy about my grandchildren, and they are crazy about pancakes for breakfast. I have become the best fast-order pancake maker around (so they tell me). I think part of the appeal is the element of danger when it comes to tossing – there is nothing like a mis-directed pancake landing on someone's head to start the day with a laugh! This is the foolproof recipe I use.

The secret is to make the batter the night before. Simply combine all the ingredients in a blender and leave in the fridge overnight. When ready to cook, brush a small omelette pan with a little butter and get it really hot. Pour in a table-spoon of the pancake mixture and swirl around quickly, to coat the bottom of the pan. When firm, flip it over and cook the other side. Toss for effect and hey-presto! (The first one is never the best so eat it yourself – you'll need it to keep going with the demand.)

Serve with your favourite fillings.

CELEBRATION BREAKFAST

Serves 2

2 hard-boiled eggs
2 eggs
2 tablespoons double cream
salt
freshly ground black pepper
knob of butter
2 heaped teaspoons caviar (or 'mock caviar')

Taking great care, tap the ends of the boiled eggs and cut around the top edge to remove a small neat slice (or use an egg slicer). Scoop out the egg and use for another dish.

Beat the raw eggs with the cream and salt and pepper. Melt the butter in a small pan. Add the egg mixture and cook, over a gentle heat, until creamy and scrambled. Quickly spoon into the egg shells and set in an egg cup. Top each with a spoonful of the caviar and serve at once with buttered toast soldiers (and a glass of champagne, if trying to impress!).

* Mark Birley is probably one of the most stylish men I've ever met. These eggs are served at Mark's Club and are my very favourite thing to eat.

MIDWAY

Midway through the day most people think of eating something, even if it's just an apple with a piece of cheese. I think we are too rigidly conditioned to set meal times, often eating from habit rather than hunger – so here are some of our ideas for people who are disinclined to be slaves to convention. These are recipes from the three of us, for the middle of the day – but also try them for supper, as a first course or a late-night snack.

Some of these recipes are very quick and are ideal for when you want a light snack. Others are more substantial and take a little more preparation and are perhaps more suitable for the weekends when you have more time. All three of us find ourselves entertaining quite a bit at weekends. Weekend eating can be given more attention, friends linger, and the meal can happily drift on.

Nanette

CHICKEN BAGUETTES

Serves 4-6

1 large French loaf
100 g (4 oz) Cambazola cheese, sliced
1 bunch of watercress, chopped
225 g (8 oz) cooked chicken, thinly sliced
2 large tomatoes, chopped
1 red onion, sliced
olive oil
salt
freshly ground black pepper

These sandwiches are perfect for picnics or weekend lunches, especially when served with iced beer or Pimms.

Slice the French loaf in half lengthways. Top one slice of the loaf with the watercress, cheese, chicken, tomatoes and onion.

Just before serving, drizzle with a little olive oil, season with salt and pepper to taste. Cover with the second slice of bread and press together gently.

Serve cut into thick wedges.

TUNA WITH APPLE SANDWICHES

Makes 8

200 g (7 oz) tuna, in brine
2 sticks of celery, chopped
2 dessert apples, chopped
2 hard-boiled eggs, chopped
1 bunch of watercress, chopped
1 bunch of spring onions, trimmed and chopped
2 teaspoons capers
2 tablespoons mayonnaise
salt
freshly ground black pepper
1 large French loaf

Flake the tuna into a bowl. Add the celery, apples, eggs, watercress, spring onions and capers, mixing well. Fold in the mayonnaise with a dash of salt and pepper.

Slice the French loaf in half lengthways. Toast the cut sides under a preheated hot grill. Cut each slice into about 4 pieces. Pile the tuna mixture onto each slice.

If you make these with fresh, grilled tuna, they are even more delicious.

GAZPACHO

Having tried many recipes for Gazpacho, I think this is the best one because it is very fresh tasting. I hate Gazpacho that looks sludgy – this one doesn't.

Serves 6

900 ml (1½ pints) tomato juice
dash of Worcestershire sauce
3 tablespoons white wine vinegar
2 tablespoons olive oil
juice of ½ lemon
salt
freshly ground black pepper
1 garlic clove, finely chopped
1 thickish slice crustless bread (brown or white)

pinch of chives or basil
½ green pepper, cored, seeded and chopped
½ red pepper, cored, seeded and chopped
½ yellow or orange pepper, cored, seeded and chopped
½ cucumber, peeled, deseeded and chopped
1 bunch of spring onions, chopped
2 tomatoes, skinned, seeded and chopped
3 sticks celery (inside ones), chopped

In a bowl mix the tomato juice, Worcestershire sauce, vinegar, oil and lemon juice. Add a few grinds of black pepper, a little salt and the garlic.

Whizz the bread and herbs in a food processor or chop until fine. Add to the liquid mixture and stir well. Add all the chopped vegetables and stir, or whizz together in the food processor. Combine the two mixtures and stir well. Chill thoroughly before serving.

I suggest you serve in large wine glasses with chunks of lightly toasted granary bread or sprinkled with freshly made croutons.

CHEAT'S GAZPACHO: When you have a lot of salad left over (made out of the usual things — lettuce, peppers, tomatoes, cucumber etc.) whisk everything in a blender, stir in some tomato juice, some extra seasoning and Worcestershire sauce and hey-presto!

MELON SALAD

Serves 4

2 Ogen or Charentais melons
3 kiwi fruit, peeled and sliced
½ cucumber, peeled and chopped
2 red dessert apples, cored and chopped
juice of 1 lemon
2 avocados, halved, stoned
and chopped

DRESSING:
3 tablespoons sunflower oil
1 tablespoon raspberry vinegar
2 teaspoons honey
1 tablespoon natural yoghurt
salt
freshly ground black pepper

Halve the melons, scoop out and discard the seeds. Using a melon scoop, baller or teaspoon, scoop out as much flesh as possible from each melon half and place in a bowl. Reserve the melon shells. Add the kiwi fruit to the melon with the cucumber, apples and lemon juice, cover and chill.

To make the dressing, beat the sunflower oil with the raspberry vinegar, honey and yoghurt. Season to taste with salt and pepper.

To serve, mix the chopped avocados with the fruit. Spoon over the dressing then fill the melon shells. Serve with warm granary bread.

BEVERLY HILLS LUNCH: I first had this in the Polo Lounge at the Beverly Hills Hotel — you feel healthy just looking at it. Cut a watermelon into thick slices (one slice for each guest). Place each slice on a large dinner plate and then arrange a selection of sliced fruit over the melon in an attractive pattern, like an artist's palette. I like to use sliced peaches, apples, oranges, pears, strawberries, raspberries, and black grapes. Everything needs to be peeled and all seeds removed. Add a small scoop of cottage cheese and garnish with mint. Serve each one with one with a black rye bread & cream cheese sandwich.

Nanette

AMERICAN CORN BREAD

Makes one 450-g (1-lb)
loaf or six large rolls

175 g (6 oz) yellow cornmeal
50 g (2 oz) plain flour
½ teaspoon baking powder
½ teaspoon salt
350 ml (12 fl oz) buttermilk
25 g (1 oz) butter, melted
1 egg, beaten

These two bread recipes are particular family favourites and are wonderful served with soups.

Mix the cornmeal with the flour, baking powder and salt. Add the buttermilk, butter and egg and beat to a smooth batter. Pour into a well-greased 450-g (1-lb) loaf tin or individual ramekin dishes. Bake in a preheated oven, 200°C/400°F (gas mark 6), for about 20 minutes.
Cool on a wire rack.

MEXICAN GREEN CHILLI CORN BREAD

Makes one 450-g
(1-lb) loaf

225 g (8 oz) plain flour
225 g (8 oz) butter
175 g (6 oz) sugar
4 eggs
350 g (12 oz) cream-style corn
100 g (4 oz) grated Cheddar
cheese
1 small tin (about 100 g/4 oz)
green chillies, diced
225 g (8 oz) plain flour
225 g (8 oz) yellow corn meal
2 level dessertspoons baking
powder
1 tablespoon salt

Cream the butter with the sugar until pale and smooth. Beat in the eggs, one at a time, mixing well. Add the cream-style corn, cheese and chillies.
In a separate bowl, sift together the flour, corn meal and baking powder. Add the salt and combine with egg mixture, mixing thoroughly.
Pour into a well-buttered 23-cm (9-inch) square tin. Bake in a preheated oven, 190°C/375°F (gas mark 5), for about 1 hour. The best way to check if this is cooked is to insert a skewer. If the skewer comes out clean, this delicious bread is ready.

Don't touch anything when you've diced the chillies. Wash your hands!

PEAR AND PEA SOUP

2 sticks celery, finely chopped
2 onions, finely chopped
50 g (2 oz) butter
1 large, ripe pear (or two if
small)
900 ml (1½ pints) vegetable or
chicken stock
350 g (¾ lb) peas (frozen are
fine)
salt and pepper
150 ml (¼ pint) cream

Gently cook the celery and onion in butter until soft but not brown. Add the pear (peeled and chopped). Cook for a few minutes until the pear is softened. Stir in the stock and simmer for about 20 minutes.

Add peas and simmer for a further 10 minutes. Take off the heat and purée in blender. Add salt and pepper. If you think it's too thick, add a little more stock. Add the cream and whirl in the blender again.

You can serve this hot or cold, sprinkled with chopped fresh mint.

STUFFED PASTA SHELLS

Serves 2-3

1 tablespoon olive oil
8-10 large pasta shells
350 g (12 oz) curd cheese
75 g (3 oz) Edam cheese,
grated
1 egg, beaten
pinch of ground paprika
salt
freshly ground black pepper
chopped fresh parsley

This is a rich but delicious pasta dish. Serve it with a plain green salad or simple grilled fish.

Bring a large pan of water to the boil and add the olive oil and the pasta. Boil briskly, uncovered, for about 8 minutes (or according to the packet instructions), until the pasta shells are cooked *al dente*. Rinse in cold water and drain thoroughly.

Mix the curd cheese with the Edam cheese, egg, paprika and salt and pepper. Carefully fill the shells with the cheese mixture and place in a buttered ovenproof baking dish. Cover with foil and bake in a preheated oven, 180°C/350°F (gas mark 4), for 15 minutes. Remove the foil and cook for a further 5 minutes. Serve at once sprinkled with chopped fresh parsley.

SPICY TOMATO AND ROCKET PASTA

John spent six weeks working in Italy and came back determined to master the art of cooking pasta. It has taken him a long time, a lot of pans, injections of Valium and whisky, but the results are sensational! (For old hats in the kitchen this is a fast sauce!)

Serves 4 (generously)

4 tablespoons olive oil
3 cloves of garlic, peeled and crushed
½ teaspoon crushed dried red chilli pepper
425 g (15 oz) can Italian plum tomatoes, deseeded and puréed

2 teaspoons tomato purée
salt
3 bunches rocket or watercress, trimmed
450 g (1 lb) spaghetti or angel-hair pasta
freshly grated Parmesan cheese to serve

Heat 3 tablespoons of the oil in a large pan. Add the garlic and red chilli pepper and cook for a few minutes. Add the puréed tomatoes, tomato purée and salt, stir thoroughly. Bring to the boil, reduce the heat and simmer gently until the sauce is thickened, about 20 minutes, stirring occasionally.

Bring a large pan of water to the boil and add the remaining olive oil and pasta.

Boil briskly, uncovered, for about 6-8 minutes (or according to the packet instructions), until the pasta is cooked *al dente*. Drain thoroughly.

Place the pasta in a large serving bowl with the rocket or watercress and sauce. Toss lightly to mix and serve at once with Parmesan cheese.

Serve with a green salad tossed in a light vinaigrette dressing.

An Italian friend suggests adding a small bunch of fresh basil to the water when cooking the pasta. Why not try it?

Spicy Tomato and Rocket Pasta

ALL-IN-ONE SALMON AND RICE

Serves 4-6

About 350 g (12 oz) cooked rice (wild is so much tastier)
450 g (1 lb) salmon, skinned and de-boned
150 ml (¼ pint) double cream
1 bunch spring onions, chopped

50 g (2 oz) butter
2 scant teaspoons curry powder (mild)
juice of 1 lemon
chopped parsley

Cut the salmon into bite-size pieces and squeeze the juice from the lemon over the salmon. Gently fry the spring onions in half of the butter until soft. Add the curry powder and stir around for about 1 minute. Add the cream and simmer gently for a couple of minutes.

In a separate pan cook the salmon pieces in butter over a very gentle heat. Add the onion and cream mixture to the rice, and stir well. Finally, add the salmon and mix gently until all the ingredients are heated through.

Sprinkle with chopped parsley to serve.

SUMMER RICE AND VEGETABLE RING: Mix some warm, cooked rice with chopped spring onion, a small amount of chopped red onion, chopped celery, cucumber, pepper (any colour), grated carrot, finely chopped raw courgette, some baby sugar snap peas, fresh herbs of your choice, and some sultanas. Then stir in some vinaigrette dressing (preferably made with walnut oil). Press gently into a ring mould or pudding bowl, cover and put in fridge. Turn out and garnish with some walnuts that have been lightly toasted in the oven for about 10 minutes.

Nanette

RISOTTO WITH FRESH PEAS

This is a great comfort food when you've been ill and are on the way to recovery. I also make this dish for my vegetarian friends.

Serves 4-6

50 g (2 oz) unsalted butter
3 medium shallots, peeled and finely chopped
225 g (8 oz) Italian risotto rice
900 ml (1½ pints) hot chicken or vegetable stock
(or canned chicken or vegetable broth)

350 g (12 oz) shelled fresh peas
100 g (4 oz) button mushrooms, wiped and sliced
salt
freshly ground black pepper
3 tablespoons freshly shaved Parmesan cheese

Melt half of the butter in a large shallow pan. Add the shallots and sauté until soft. Stir in the rice, mixing well and cook for 2 minutes but don't let it brown.

Add the peas and 120 ml (4 fl oz) of the stock or broth. Simmer gently until it has been absorbed by the rice. Add the remaining stock, about 120 ml (4 fl oz) at a time, until it has all been absorbed by the rice – stop when the rice is cooked and just tender (don't let it go mushy whatever you do). Meanwhile, melt the remaining butter in a small pan. Add the mushrooms and cook until lightly browned. Add to the cooked rice with salt and pepper. Stir and gently fold in the Parmesan cheese and serve at once.

This is a delicious lunch dish on its own or as an accompaniment to meat.

Sometimes I leave out the mushrooms altogether and replace with 75 g (3 oz) fresh pesto. It gives this risotto a wonderful green colour.

SOUFFLÉ PIE

Serves 4-6

a few fresh breadcrumbs
100 g (4 oz) butter
6 eggs, separated
225 g (8 oz) cooked asparagus
tips
275 g (10 oz) Cheddar cheese,
grated
1 teaspoon salt
1 tablespoon chopped fresh
parsley
¼ teaspoon cayenne pepper

This isn't quite a soufflé and it isn't quite a pie – but it is a nice light dish to have with a salad.

Lightly butter a 25- x 15-cm (10- x 6-inch) ovenproof dish and coat with breadcrumbs. Beat the butter and egg yolks in a blender or food processor until pale and fluffy. Stir in the asparagus tips, cheese, salt, parsley and cayenne pepper.

Whisk the egg whites until they stand in stiff peaks. Fold into the cheese mixture. Pour into the prepared dish and bake in a preheated oven, 180°C/350°F (gas mark 4), for 35 minutes, or until puffy and pale brown.

Serve at once.

DUCK AND ORANGE SALAD

Serves 4

4 cooked duck breast fillets,
skinned and cut into thin strips
4 oranges, peeled, pith removed
and segmented
1 bunch of watercress, chopped
1 small radicchio lettuce,
trimmed

DRESSING:
3 tablespoons sunflower oil
1 tablespoon fresh orange juice
½ teaspoon wholegrain mustard
1 tablespoon chopped fresh
chives
salt
freshly ground black pepper

Mix the duck with the oranges and watercress. Arrange on one large or four individual serving plates on a bed of radicchio leaves.

To make the dressing, beat the oil with the orange juice, mustard, chives and salt and pepper to taste. Just before serving spoon over the salad.

Why don't you try using pink grapefruit instead of orange?

CHILLED MONKFISH WITH PEARS

Leave the garlic out of this dish if you are in love.

Serves 3-4

450 g (1 lb) monkfish fillets, skinned and cubed
150 ml (¼ pint) water
1 tablespoon lemon juice
salt
freshly ground white pepper
2 dessert pears, peeled, cored and thinly sliced
50 g (2 oz) pine nuts
2 handfuls lambs' lettuce

DRESSING:
5 tablespoons olive oil
1 tablespoon white wine vinegar
2 tablespoons chopped fresh tarragon
1 clove of garlic, peeled and crushed
quartered lemon slices

Poach the monkfish in the water and lemon juice with salt and pepper until just tender, about 5 minutes. Drain and cool then chill thoroughly.

Mix the monkfish with the pear slices, pine nuts and lambs' lettuce in a serving bowl or on a large shallow plate.

To make the dressing, blend the oil with the vinegar, tarragon, garlic and salt and pepper to taste. Spoon over the salad and toss gently.

Serve with quartered lemon slices.

SPECIAL SMOKED SALAD

Followed by fresh fruit and coffee, this makes a delicious light lunch. What could be nicer?

Serves 4

2 smoked chicken or turkey breasts, skinned and cut into thin strips
1 yellow pepper cored, seeded and cut into thin strips
6 spring onions, trimmed and cut lengthways into 2 cm (1 inch) diagonal strips
2 bunches of watercress or baby spinach leaves, finely chopped

225 g (8 oz) small new potatoes, cooked
225 g (8 oz) can lychees, drained
4 tablespoons soured cream
4 tablespoons mayonnaise
1 tablespoon fresh tarragon, finely chopped
salt
freshly ground black pepper

Mix the smoked chicken or turkey breast with the pepper strips, spring onions, chopped watercress, new potatoes and lychees.

Blend the soured cream with the mayonnaise, tarragon and salt and pepper. Fold into the chicken mixture. Spoon the salad onto a large serving plate and chill.

This is one of those recipes you can mess around with. Why not try adding crisp, blanched French beans or asparagus.

Special Smoked Salad

ENGLISH-STYLE RED FLANNEL HASH

This is very American and is often eaten for breakfast with an egg on the top. It also makes a delicious lunch dish. This is my slightly anglicised version.

Serves 4-6

50 g (2 oz) butter
1 red onion, peeled and chopped
3 large boiled potatoes, diced
700 g (1½ lb) corned beef, chopped
1 large cooked beetroot, peeled and chopped

150 ml (¼ pint) soured cream
2 tablespoons chopped fresh chives
dash of Worcestershire sauce
2 hard-boiled eggs, shelled and chopped
salt

Melt the butter in a large heavy-based frying pan. Add the onion and cook until softened, about 5 minutes. Add the potatoes and cook for a few minutes, stirring occasionally.

Add the corned beef and stir, over a low heat, until the mixture is very hot.

Add the beetroot and stir around for a minute more.

Meanwhile, mix the soured cream with the chives and Worcestershire sauce. Fold in the hard-boiled egg with salt and pepper. Fold the soured cream mixture into the hot hash. Serve at once.

UP-MARKET BEANS ON TOAST: Peel and chop 4 large cloves of garlic, 2 small red onions and 2 shallots. Put in a shallow roasting tray with 2 tins of drained cannelloni beans, about 30 halved cherry tomatoes, 8 tablespoons of olive oil and a pinch of dried basil. Stir thoroughly. Season with salt and pepper and roast in a preheated medium oven for about 30-40 minutes. Serve on toasted Italian bread with salad. Will serve 10 as a first course or 6 as a main course.

Sarah

SAVOURY QUICHE PASTRY

Makes 1 quantity pastry
(enough to line a 20- to
23-cm/8- to 9-inch quiche
tin or dish)

175 g (6 oz) plain flour
pinch of salt
100 g (4 oz) butter
1 egg
1 tablespoon iced water
2 teaspoons lemon juice

Everyone has a favourite way of making pastry – here is ours:

Put the flour, salt and butter in a food processor and process until the mixture resembles fine breadcrumbs. Beat the egg with the water and lemon juice. Add to the dry ingredients with the motor running and process just until the mixture forms a ball. Wrap in clingfilm and chill for 30-40 minutes before using.

Alternatively, if you wish to make it by hand, sift the flour with the salt into a bowl. Rub in the butter until the mixture resembles fine breadcrumbs. Beat the egg with the water and lemon juice. Add to the dry ingredients and mix to a smooth dough. Knead lightly then wrap in clingfilm and chill for 30-40 minutes before using.

— *Nanette* —

UNCOMPLICATED CRAB PIE

Serves 4

1 quantity Savoury Quiche
Pastry (above)
3 eggs
175 ml (6 fl oz) single cream
1 tablespoon chopped fresh
parsley
225 g (8 oz) crabmeat, flaked
salt
freshly ground black pepper

This is the simplest of pies and needs nothing more than a green salad to go with it.

Roll out the pastry on a lightly floured surface and use to line a 23-cm (9-inch) flan dish or tin. Prick the pastry and bake 'blind' in a preheated oven, 200°C/400°F (gas mark 6), for 10 minutes. Remove and reduce the oven temperature to 180°C/350°F (gas mark 4).

Beat the eggs with the cream, parsley, crabmeat and salt and pepper and spoon into the pastry case. Return to the oven and bake for about 40 minutes or until the filling is firm and the pastry is crisp and golden.

Serve warm or cold.

TOMATO AND MOZZARELLA TART

These quantities are for six people – I usually double the amount since people always want second helpings! You can smell the garlic as you come up the drive.

Serves 6

200 g (7 oz) plain flour
175 g (6 oz) butter, chilled
1 tablespoon sugar
salt
3-4 tablespoons iced water
3-4 tablespoons Dijon mustard

450 g (1 lb) Mozzarella cheese, thinly sliced
10 large tomatoes, skinned and sliced
1 teaspoon dried oregano
2 tablespoons chopped garlic
freshly ground black pepper
2 tablespoons olive oil

To make the base, sift the flour into a bowl, then rub in the butter until the mixture resembles fine breadcrumbs. Stir in the sugar, a pinch of salt and the water to make a smooth dough. Wrap in clingfilm and chill for 30 minutes.

Roll out the dough on a lightly floured surface to line a greased 25- x 20-cm (10- x 8-inch) shallow baking tin (this pastry is very fragile and not easy to roll out, so don't worry if you have to patch it together).

Spread the mustard over the pastry base and top with the sliced cheese. Cover with the sliced tomatoes, overlapping them slightly. Sprinkle with the oregano, garlic and salt and pepper. Drizzle with the oil and bake in a preheated oven, 200°C/400°F (gas mark 6), for about 40 minutes.

Halfway through the cooking time check the tart. If there are excess cooking juices, gently spoon away and return the tart to the oven.

Serve hot with a crisp green salad.

Tomato and Mozzarella Tart

ITALIAN FISH PIE

I've always called this salmon, brill and parsley fish pie 'Italian Fish Pie' because of its colours – red, white and green.

Serves 4-6

450 g (1 lb) brill fillets
450 ml (¾ pint) milk
salt
freshly ground black pepper
1 bay leaf
50 g (2 oz) butter

3 tablespoons plain flour
2 tablespoons chopped fresh parsley
225 g (8 oz) cooked salmon, flaked
2 hard-boiled eggs, shelled and cut into wedges
about 1 kg (2 lb) mashed potatoes

Poach the brill fillets in the milk with salt, pepper and the bay leaf until tender. Drain, reserving the milk and discarding the bay leaf. Skin and flake the brill fillets.

Melt three-quarters of the butter in a pan. Add the flour and cook for 1 minute. Gradually add the milk, bring to the boil, stirring until smooth and thickened. Season the sauce with salt and pepper and stir in the chopped parsley.

Mix the brill with the salmon, eggs and sauce. Spoon into a large shallow ovenproof dish. Top the pie with the mashed potatoes and dot with the remaining butter.

Bake in a preheated oven, 190°C/375°F (gas mark 5), for 30-40 minutes, or until the potato is lightly browned.

Serve hot.

A fish, simply grilled and seasoned with salt, pepper and lemon juice, really can't be beaten. If you need a simple sauce to ring the changes, try combining fresh tomatoes, spring onions, a pinch of sugar, a dash of balsamic vinegar and a dash of the best olive oil, whirled in a food processor with perhaps a little basil. This is good with most fish.

Nanette

PRAWNS IN LEMON SAUCE WITH TAGLIATELLE

Driving through Italy, we stopped at a tiny, rather tacky, roadside restaurant and were served this delicious dish.

Serves 4

1 tablespoon olive oil
350 g (12 oz) tagliatelle verdi
300 ml (½ pint) double cream
grated rind and juice of 1 lemon

salt
freshly ground white pepper
225 g (8 oz) peeled prawns
chopped fresh chervil

Bring a large pan of water to the boil and add the olive oil and the pasta. Boil briskly, uncovered, for about 6 minutes (or according to the packet instructions), until the pasta is cooked *al dente*. Drain thoroughly.

Meanwhile, place the cream, lemon rind, lemon juice and salt and pepper in a pan and bring to the boil. Reduce the heat and cook gently until the sauce thickens. Add the prawns and heat through.

Mix the sauce with the pasta and sprinkle with chervil.

Serve at once.

This is so delicious and so simple: Slice an aubergine into 1-cm (¼-inch) slices. (If you have time, sprinkle the slices with salt, leave for a couple of hours to drain away any bitter juices and then rinse and pat dry.) Mix together some wholemeal breadcrumbs and grated Parmesan cheese. Spread the aubergine slices with mayonnaise and coat with the breadcrumb mixture. Season lightly and bake in a moderate oven until nicely brown (about 15 minutes).

Nanette

TOTALLY SIMPLE SEA BASS

Serves 4-6

2.75 kg (6 lb) sea bass, cleaned and scaled
fresh fennel or dill sprigs
salt

freshly ground black pepper
juice of 2 lemons
2 tablespoons olive oil

Using a sharp knife, cut deep diagonal slashes into the flesh of the bass and insert springs of fresh fennel or dill. Season the inside of the fish with salt and pepper and stuff with more fresh fennel or dill. Season the outside of the fish with salt and pepper and squeeze over half of the lemon juice and olive oil.

Cook under a preheated hot grill until the flesh is cooked. Turn over carefully and squeeze over the remaining lemon juice and olive oil. Return to the grill and cook until the flesh is tender.

Serve hot with any cooking juices poured over the fish and with extra chunks of lemon.

Sardines make the whole house smell so strongly that although they are delicious to eat, you sometimes wonder whether it is worth ever cooking them. They are however, perfect for barbecues. If you feel you need more than just lashings of lemon to serve with them, try this: Whirl in a blender 3 medium tomatoes (skinned), 6 small onions, a handful of fresh basil, a piece of skinned cucumber, a tablespoon of olive oil and a teaspoon of balsamic vinegar until smooth.

Nanette

SMOKED GINGERED FILO TROUT

Serves 4

2 smoked trout, skinned, boned and flaked
juice of 1 lemon
2.5 cm (1 in) piece root ginger, peeled and grated
1 large tomato, skinned, seeded and cut into strips
3 tablespoons crème fraîche

2 teaspoons creamed horseradish
1 teaspoon chopped fresh dill
salt
freshly ground black pepper
12 sheets filo pastry
50 g (2 oz) butter, melted

Put the trout in a shallow dish and sprinkle over the lemon juice. Add the ginger and tomatoes, mixing well. Cover and leave to stand for 15 minutes. Stir in the crème fraîche, horseradish, dill and salt and pepper.

Lay out 4 sheets of the filo pastry and brush each with a little of the melted butter. Cover each with another sheet of pastry and brush again with melted butter.

Repeat twice until you have used up all the filo pastry sheets.

Divide the trout mixture evenly between the pastry piles. Carefully fold into parcels to enclose the filling and brush with any remaining butter. Place each, seam-side down, on a baking tray and bake in a preheated oven, 190°C/375°F (Gas mark 5), for 15-20 minutes, until pale brown and crisp.

Make simple grilled fish into something more interesting by serving it with this SAUCE FOR WHITE FISH. Remove the hard stems from 1 kg (2 lb) sorrel. Chop finely and cook gently in 40 g (1½ oz) butter until softened, stirring all the time. Add 100 ml (4 fl oz) double cream and salt and pepper to taste. Cook over a very low heat for 2-3 minutes until slightly thickened. Stir in 100 ml (4 fl oz) natural yoghurt and cook for ½ minute. Serve warm. Serves 4-6.

— *Nanette* —

COATED RED MULLET

Serves 6

50 g (2 oz) butter
75 g (3 oz) chopped fresh herbs
of your choice
6 medium red mullet, cleaned
and heads removed
25 g (1 oz) plain flour
250 ml (8 fl oz) dry white wine
juice of 2 lemons

Melt the butter in a large pan. Add the herbs and cook gently for 1 minute. Coat the fish in the flour and add to the pan. Cook gently in the butter mixture for 2 minutes on each side.

Add the wine and lemon juice and transfer the fish and juice to a shallow ovenproof dish. Cover and bake in a preheated oven, 180°C/350°F (gas mark 4), for 15 minutes. Remove and place under a preheated hot grill until golden brown and bubbly.

Serve at once.

— *Emma* —

BAKED COD

Serves 4-6

1.125 kg (2½ lb) cod (or
halibut or any other
firm white fish), skinned and
cubed
3 slices streaky bacon
2 tablespoons olive oil
1 large onion, chopped
400 g (14 oz) can tomatoes,
drained and chopped
chopped parsley
salt
freshly ground black pepper
a few black, pitted olives
2 level dessertspoons capers
thick slice of bread

Place the fish in a large, buttered ovenproof dish. In a pan, sauté the chopped bacon in the olive oil until crisp. Add the onion and cook till soft. Add the tomatoes and simmer for about 20 minutes. Add the parsley, salt, pepper, olives and capers and stir thoroughly. Pour over the fish. Cover, and bake in a preheated oven, 180°C/350°F (gas mark 4), for about 20 minutes, or until the fish is cooked and flakes easily with a fork. Quickly sauté some cubes of bread in butter. Drain, and sprinkle over the top of the fish before serving.

Coated Red Mullet

CHICKEN WITH APRICOT AND RICE STUFFING

This is simply an interesting version of roast chicken. Serve with steamed young broccoli.

Serves 4-6

1.6-1.8 kg (3½-4 lb) oven-ready chicken
1 tablespoon sunflower oil
a handful of fresh lemon balm or parsley
2 teaspoons cornflour
juice of 2 oranges

STUFFING:
50 g (2 oz) long-grain rice, cooked
50 g (2 oz) dried apricots, finely chopped
2 sticks of celery, finely chopped
50 g (2 oz) pine nuts, toasted
50 g (2 oz) sultanas
salt
freshly ground black pepper
2 tablespoons natural yoghurt
2 tablespoons chopped fresh tarragon

Rinse the chicken inside and out with cold water then pat dry with absorbent paper.

To make the stuffing, mix the cooked rice with the apricots, celery, pine nuts, sultanas and salt and pepper to taste. Bind together with the yoghurt and tarragon. Spoon the stuffing into the body cavity of the chicken and truss with string to secure.

Put the chicken in the roasting pan and brush with the sunflower oil. Sprinkle with a little salt then cover with the fresh lemon balm or parsley.

Roast in a preheated oven, 190°C/375°F (gas mark 5), for 1¼-1½ hours, basting frequently with the pan juices, until the chicken is cooked and the juices run clear. Remove from the oven and transfer to a warmed serving plate. Keep warm.

Dissolve the cornflour in the orange juice and stir into the pan juices. Bring to the boil, stirring until smooth and thickened. If the sauce seems too thick at this stage, then add 2 tablespoons water to thin to your taste.

Serve with any green vegetable.

GRAHAM'S HOT/COLD CHICKEN SALAD

Graham rarely goes in to the kitchen to cook anything. This is his one and only dish which he needs an assistant to help create – normally me! It's not for those who are dieting or watching their cholesterol!

Serves 4-6

2 tablespoons sunflower oil
6 chicken breasts, skinned, boned and cut into strips
250 ml (8 fl oz) mayonnaise
300 g (10 oz) can waterchestnuts, drained and chopped
4 sticks of celery, chopped

50 g (2 oz) flaked almonds
salt
freshly ground black pepper
juice of 1 lemon
1 family pack of salted crisps
100 g (4 oz) Cheddar cheese, grated

Heat the oil in a frying pan and sauté the chicken until lightly browned. Remove with a slotted spoon and mix with the mayonnaise, waterchestnuts, celery, almonds, salt, pepper and lemon juice. Spoon into a shallow casserole dish.

Lightly crush the crisps and mix with the cheese. Scatter over the chicken mixture, cover with foil and bake in a preheated oven, 180°C/350°F (gas mark 4), for 30-40 minutes until the chicken is completely cooked through.

Remove the foil and grill until the cheese is golden brown.

Serve at once with a crisp green salad and interesting bread.

CHESTNUT CHICKEN

I prefer boned chicken because it's so easy to carve. This is a very English stuffing.

Serves 6

1.6-1.8 kg (3½-4 lb) oven-ready chicken, boned
150 ml (¼ pint) stock
6-8 slices white or wholemeal bread
100 g (4 oz) butter
1 large onion, peeled and chopped
½ x 312 g (11 oz) can unsweetened whole
chestnuts, drained and chopped

1 tablespoon chopped fresh tarragon
1 tablespoon chopped fresh parsley
1 egg, beaten
sea salt
freshly ground black pepper
1 tablespoon sunflower oil
fresh parsley sprigs

Place the chicken, skin-side down, on a large board. Turn the legs and the wings of the chicken inside out. Pour the stock over the bread and leave to soak.

Melt the butter in a pan. Add the onion and sauté until softened. Remove from the heat and mix in the soaked bread, chestnuts, tarragon, parsley, egg and salt and pepper.

Spread the stuffing mixture over the chicken, draw the sides of the bird together and sew up (using a trussing needle and fine thread) to a good shape. Place in a roasting tray and brush with the sunflower oil. Season with salt and pepper. Roast in a preheated oven, 190°C/375°F (gas mark 5), for about 1¾ hours, until the chicken is cooked.

Remove the thread. Serve hot or cold with vegetables (for example, French beans and carrots) or a salad. Garnish with fresh parsley sprigs.

In the summer try cooking a plain roast chicken and serving it hot with a cold, very minty, vinaigrette dressing — very interesting, very delicious and very easy.
Nanette

Chestnut Chicken, Steamed Carrots with Fennel and Hazelnuts (page 127)

LAMB WITH ROSEMARY AND GARLIC

Serves 6-8

3 cloves of garlic
1.8 kg (4 lb) leg of lamb
2 tablespoons olive oil
2 teaspoons chopped fresh rosemary
½ teaspoon chopped fresh thyme

salt
freshly ground black pepper
150 ml (¼ pint) light stock
juice of 1 lemon
25 g (1 oz) butter

Peel the garlic and cut into thin slivers. Using a sharp, pointed knife or skewer, make small cuts in the lamb and insert a sliver of garlic in each. Place the lamb in a roasting pan.

Mix the olive oil with the rosemary, thyme and salt and pepper and pour over the lamb. Roast in a preheated oven, 220°C/425°F (gas mark 7), for 15 minutes. Reduce the oven temperature to 190°C/375°F (gas mark 5), and cook for a further 1¼-1¾ hours, or until the lamb is cooked but still pink towards the centre of the leg – the juices that flow from the lamb when pierced should be colourless.

Remove the meat from the roasting pan and place on a warmed serving dish. Keep warm. Add the stock to the pan, scraping all the bits. Bring to the boil and add the lemon juice and salt and pepper. Stir in the butter, cut into small pieces, blending well to make a sauce.

Serve cut into slices with a little of the sauce drizzled over.

This is delicious served with a selection of nursery style vegetable purées (for example, carrots cooked and puréed with a little potato; parsnips cooked, puréed and seasoned with a little nutmeg and cream; and broccoli cooked and puréed with a little cottage cheese).

Emma

SPICED LENTILS

This is particularly good with cold meats.

450 g (1 lb) Puy or red lentils

2 medium onions, chopped

3 cloves garlic, finely chopped

1 tablespoon sunflower oil

2 large tomatoes, chopped

¼ teaspoon chilli powder

½ teaspoon turmeric

½ teaspoon cinnamon

½ teaspoon ginger

½ teaspoon coriander

Boil the lentils with half of the onion and the garlic and turmeric powder. Season with salt. Cook until soft. Put the oil in another pan, and add the rest of the onion. Cook until translucent. Add spices and cook for another 3 minutes. Add the lentil mixture and tomatoes and cook for a further 5 minutes.

FRUIT STUFFED LAMB: Sprinkle a 2.25 kg (5 lb) flattened leg of lamb with salt and pepper. Gently cook 1 chopped onion in 2 tablespoons of butter, until just soft. Add 2 tablespoons finely chopped celery, 1 packet mixed dried fruit and ½ cup of breadcrumbs. Mix thoroughly. Spread the fruit filling over the lamb leaving about 2 cm (1 inch) around the edge. Roll up the lamb as best you can (it may pay to have another pair of hands ready!), and tie into a neat parcel. Place in a baking tin, pour over 2 tablespoons olive oil and sprinkle with sea salt. Cover with sprigs of rosemary. You could stick in some cloves of garlic if you like. Cook for about 2½ hours in a preheated oven, 180°C/350°F (gas mark 4). Halfway through cooking, add a teacupful of port, and top with a heaped tablespoon of redcurrant jelly. When cooked, leave to settle for 10 minutes or so. Serve with the juices from the tin.

Nanette

SPICY LAMB WITH YOGHURT

It is said that the way to a man's heart is through his stomach. I have never believed that. However, I do know a woman who says she fell in love with her husband because he was a superb cook. She has never, to my knowledge, set foot in her kitchen other than to make a cup of tea or coffee. After ten years she is still happily married, well fed, and a lot of her female friends can't help turning green occasionally. This was (according to him) the first thing he cooked for her.

Serves 10-12

2.75 kg (6 lb) leg of lamb

MARINADE:
6 large cloves of garlic, peeled
about a 5-cm (2-inch) piece root ginger, peeled
2 teaspoons sea salt
grated rind and juice of 1 large lemon

1 heaped teaspoon cumin powder
½ heaped teaspoon ground turmeric
1 heaped teaspoon dried rosemary
½ heaped teaspoon dried cloves
600 ml (1 pint) natural yoghurt
1½ tablespoons honey

Using a skewer, make small holes all over the surface of the lamb deep into the flesh.

Put the garlic, ginger, salt, lemon rind and juice, cumin powder, turmeric, rosemary and cloves in a blender or food processor and purée until smooth. Rub this mixture over the surface of the lamb and place in a roasting tray. Without washing the blender or food processor, add half of the yoghurt and the honey. Whirl around then pour over the lamb. Cover with foil and refrigerate overnight to thoroughly marinate the lamb.

To cook the lamb, place in a preheated oven, 220°C/425°F (gas mark 7), for 30 minutes. Reduce the oven temperature to 160°C/325°F (gas mark 3), and cook for a further 1½ hours, basting occasionally with the marinade juices. Remove the foil cover and cook for a further 30 minutes. Remove the meat from the pan and place on a warmed serving dish. Keep warm.

Stir the remaining yoghurt into the cooking juices and stir briskly over a low heat to blend. Serve hot with the lamb.

Garnish the lamb with sprigs of rosemary if liked.

This is not a recipe for those who like their lamb pink and underdone.

Spicy Lamb with Yoghurt

STAY FOR TEA

If one could ever say that certain meals have gone out of fashion, I suppose afternoon tea has. There are still some people who, at four o'clock, continue the time-honoured ritual, but for most of us it is probably more likely to be a tea-bag in the kitchen with a packet of biscuits.

It is, however, occasionally nice to pay a bit more attention to this very English tradition. So conjure up thoughts of tea on a sun-drenched lawn, or in front of a log fire on a winter's afternoon – little sandwiches, scones, spice-scented cake. Ah well, it's pleasant to think about.

Nanette

BANANA BREAD WITH GRAPEFRUIT CREAM

This is a teabread that is marvellous served warm with butter and honey, or cold with a Grapefruit Cream Cheese Topping.

Makes one 450-g (1-lb) loaf

100 g (4 oz) butter
225 g (8 oz) soft brown sugar
grated rind of 1 small grapefruit
1 egg
2 ripe bananas, peeled and mashed
100 g (4 oz) self-raising flour
100 g (4 oz) plain wholewheat flour
1½ teaspoons baking powder
4 tablespoons natural yoghurt

GRAPEFRUIT CREAM
CHEESE TOPPING:
225 g (8 oz) cream cheese
grated rind of 1 grapefruit
2 tablespoons grapefruit juice
75 g (3 oz) icing sugar, sifted

Cream the butter with the sugar and grapefruit rind until very pale and creamy. Beat in the egg and fold in the mashed bananas.

Sift the flours with the baking powder, adding any bran left in the sieve. Fold into the banana mixture with the yoghurt. Mix very well. Spoon into a greased 450-g (1-lb) loaf tin and level the surface. Bake in a preheated oven, 180°C/350°F (gas mark 4), for 1 hour, or until a skewer inserted comes out clean.

To make the Grapefruit Cream Cheese Topping, beat the cream cheese with the grapefruit rind, grapefruit juice and icing sugar to make a smooth icing. When the banana bread is completely cool, swirl over the bread.

PRUNE CAKE

Makes one 900-g
(2-lb) loaf

175 g (6 oz) prunes, chopped
225 g (8 oz) plain flour
2 teaspoons baking powder
1 teaspoon ground mixed spice
75 g (3 oz) butter
75 ml (3 fl oz) maple syrup
75 g (3 oz) orange marmalade
100 g (4 oz) Demerara sugar
150 ml (¼ pint) milk
1 egg, beaten
50 g (2 oz) chopped apple
50 g (2 oz) broken pecan nuts
1 tablespoon brown rum

Cook the prunes in a little water until soft. Cool then chop. Sift the flour with the baking powder and mixed spice.

Melt the butter in a large pan with the maple syrup, marmalade and sugar. Add the flour mixture, milk and egg and mix. Stir in the prunes, apple and pecan nuts.

Spoon into a greased 900-g (2-lb) loaf tin. Bake in a preheated oven, 180°C/350°F (gas mark 4), for 1-1¼ hours, or until a skewer inserted comes out clean.

Remove from the tin while still warm. Poke holes using a skewer in the base of the cake and pour over the rum. Leave to cool.

WALNUT CAKE

Makes one 20-cm (8-inch)
round cake

250 ml (8 fl oz) double cream
2 eggs, lightly beaten
225 g (8 oz) caster sugar
50 g (2 oz) ground walnuts
150 g (5 oz) plain flour
2 teaspoons baking powder
pinch of salt

TOPPING:
25 g (1 oz) butter
1 tablespoon double cream
60 g (2½ oz) caster sugar
1 tablespoon flour
25 g (1 oz) walnuts

Whip the cream until it stands in soft peaks. Gradually add the eggs and sugar, beating all the time. Stir in the walnuts. Sift the flour with the baking powder and salt and fold into the creamed mixture.

Pour into a greased and floured 20-cm (8-inch) diameter spring-form cake tin. Bake in a preheated oven, 180°C/350°F (gas mark 4), for 1-1¼ hours; it should feel firm and springy.

To make the topping, melt the butter with the cream, sugar, flour and walnuts in a small pan. Remove the cake from the oven and pour over the walnut mixture to cover. Return to the oven to cook for a further 10 minutes.

Cool slightly in the tin before removing.

From left to right clockwise: Soured Cream Pound Cake (page 59), Citrus Cake (page 60), Pistachio Cookies (page 67)

CARROT AND BRANDY CAKE

There are so many types of carrot cake – I try lots of them but always come back to this one. It is very moist and is also superb as a dessert served with crème fraîche or for tea just plain. I've given a recipe for an optional icing, but really I think it's gilding the lily.

Makes one 23- to 25-cm (9- to 10-inch) cake

225 g (8 oz) carrots, peeled and sliced
6 eggs, separated
225 g (8 oz) sugar
1 heaped tablespoon grated raw carrot
grated rind of 1 large orange
350 g (12 oz) ground almonds
1 tablespoon brandy (or fresh orange juice)

ICING:
225 g (8 oz) cream cheese
6 tablespoons icing sugar, sifted
2 tablespoons concentrated frozen orange juice

Cook the carrots in boiling water until very soft. Drain and purée in a blender or food processor until smooth. Beat the egg yolks with the sugar until very pale. Add the carrot purée, grated carrot, orange rind, almonds and brandy or orange juice, blending well. Whisk the egg whites until they stand in stiff peaks and fold into the carrot mixture. Pour into a greased loose-bottomed 23- to 25-cm (9- to 10-inch) spring-form cake tin.

Bake in a preheated oven, 160°C/325°F (gas mark 3), for about 50-60 minutes or until a skewer inserted comes out clean. Cool.

To make the icing, beat the cream cheese with the icing sugar and orange juice (there is no need to thaw it). Chill before swirling over the top of the cake.

If you have one eye on the clock and a cake to make, then try this HIGH-SPEED BROWN SUGARY CAKE: Liberally butter a 23-cm (9-inch) spring-form cake tin and spoon over 225 g (8 oz) brown sugar mixed with ½ teaspoon ground cinnamon. Put 4 eggs, 75 g (3 oz) ground almonds, 250 ml (8 fl oz) soured cream, 3 tablespoons plain flour, 225 g (8 oz) cream cheese and 2 tablespoons Grand Marnier in a food processor and blend while counting up to 20. Pour into the tin and bake in a preheated oven, 180°C/350°F (gas mark 4), for 40 minutes. Carefully remove from the tin. Serve warm or cold.

Nanette

SOURED CREAM POUND CAKE

I once ran out of the double cream this recipe usually calls for, so I used soured cream instead. It's much better and makes a wonderful dessert if served with ice cream and surrounded with fresh berries.

Makes one 900-g (2-lb) loaf, small tube or Bundt cake

100 g (4 oz) butter
100 g (4 oz) sugar
4 eggs, separated
350 g (12 oz) plain flour

pinch of salt
½ teaspoon cream of tartar
150 ml (¼ pint) soured cream mixed with
1 teaspoon vanilla essence

Grease a 900-g (2-lb) loaf tin, small tube or Bundt tin and dust lightly with flour.

Cream the butter with the sugar until pale. Add the egg yolks, one at a time, beating them in well.

Sift the flour with the salt and cream of tartar and fold into the creamed mixture alternating with the soured cream.

Whisk the egg whites until they stand in stiff mountains. Fold into the cake mixture. Spoon into the prepared tin and bake in a preheated oven, 180°C/350°F (gas mark 4), for 1¼-1½ hours, or until a skewer inserted comes out clean. Cool on a wire rack.

If you can't ice a cake for a special occasion, you can still make it look wonderful. Join together three or four helium-filled balloons halfway down their strings, then attach the string to a small wooden skewer and plunge into the cake. Add an extravagant ribbon. You'll be surprised how impressed everyone will be.

Emma

CITRUS CAKE

Makes one 20-cm (8-inch) sandwich cake

CAKE:
175 g (6 oz) butter
175 g (6 oz) caster sugar
3 eggs, beaten
finely grated rind of 1 lemon
175 g (6 oz) self-raising flour

FILLING:
3 tablespoons cornflour
3 tablespoons lemon juice
150 g (5 oz) caster sugar
125 ml (4 ½ fl oz) orange juice
finely-grated rind of 1 lemon
15 g (½ oz) butter
3 egg yolks, lightly beaten
150 ml (¼ pint) double cream
strips of lemon zest to decorate

Grease the bases of two 20-cm (8-inch) sandwich tins and line with greaseproof paper.

Cream the butter with the sugar until pale and fluffy. Add the eggs, a little at a time, mixing well. Fold in the lemon rind and flour. Divide the mixture between the prepared tins and bake in a preheated oven, 190°C/375°F (gas mark 5), for 20 minutes, until firm to the touch.

Cool slightly in the tins then transfer to a wire rack.

To make the filling, mix the cornflour with the lemon juice. Place the sugar, orange juice, lemon rind and butter in a heatproof bowl over a pan of boiling water.

Add the cornflour mixture. Cook for 5 minutes, stirring constantly, then cook for a further 10 minutes without stirring. Remove the bowl from the heat and stir in the egg yolks. Return to the heat for a further 5-10 minutes, or until the mixture thickens. Remove from the heat and cool, stirring occasionally.

Use two-thirds of the filling to sandwich the cake layers together. Spread the remaining filling over the top of the cake and swirl with a palette knife.

Whip the cream until it stands in soft peaks. Swirl around the edges of the cake and decorate the edges with strips of lemon zest.

APPLE SAUCE CAKE

Makes one 19-cm (7½-inch) sandwich cake

225 g (8 oz) plain flour
1½ teaspoons bicarbonate of soda
½ teaspoon salt
2 teaspoons ground cinnamon
¼ teaspoon ground nutmeg
150 g (5 oz) butter
225 g (8 oz) caster sugar
2 eggs, beaten
225 g (8 oz) apple purée or canned apple sauce

40 g (1½ oz) sultanas
40 g (1½ oz) raisins
75 g (3 oz) walnuts, coarsely chopped

ICING:
100 g (4 oz) ricotta cheese
75 g (3 oz) icing sugar, sifted
juice of 1 lime

Grease the bases of two 19-cm (7 ½-inch) sandwich tins and line with greaseproof paper.

Sift the flour with the bicarbonate of soda, salt, cinnamon and nutmeg. Cream the butter with the sugar until pale and fluffy. Beat in the eggs, a little at a time, adding a small amount of the flour if the mixture begins to curdle. Fold in the remaining flour with the apple purée, sultanas, raisins and walnuts.

Divide the mixture and spoon into the cake tins. Bake in a preheated oven, 180°C/350°F (gas mark 4), for 30 minutes, or until well-risen and firm. Cool for a few minutes then turn out onto a wire rack.

For the icing, beat the ricotta until smooth and creamy. Gradually add the icing sugar with the lime juice, beating all the time to make a smooth icing. Sandwich the apple sauce cake layers together with the icing.

Nothing tastes better than your own HOME-MADE LEMON CURD. It is simple to make and is delicious on toast, in tarts or over ice cream. Gently cook 6 lightly beaten egg yolks with 225 g (8 oz) caster sugar and 100 ml (4 fl oz) freshly squeezed lemon juice until the mixture coats the back of a spoon. Gradually beat in 100 g (4 oz) softened butter then pot in sterilised jars. Seal, label and store in the refrigerator for up to 3 weeks.

Nanette

LOXTON'S AMAZING CAKE
(OR PUDDING!)

Our doctor's wife, Mary, makes this cake and although all of us have always boasted that we have the best chocolate cake recipe, we've finally had to admit – THIS is the best. So here it is. It's very versatile – you can serve it as a cake, or as a pudding, with crème fraîche or ice-cream. In case you're wondering, yes, it is fattening.

225 g (8 oz) best dark chocolate
225 g (8 oz) soft brown sugar
225 g (8 oz) butter

6 eggs
225 g (8 oz) ground almonds
225 g (8 oz) white breadcrumbs

Melt chocolate in a bowl over a pan of simmering water. In a separate bowl, beat the butter and sugar until pale. Add the eggs one at a time – they will look curdled but don't worry. Add the chocolate, almonds and breadcrumbs and mix thoroughly. Bake in two 21-cm (8½-in) tins at 190°C/375°F (gas mark 5), for 20-25 minutes (or until just moist in the middle and firm on the edges).

When cooled, sandwich the two cakes together with your favourite chocolate filling. Ours is: Melt 100 g (4 oz) butter and 100 g (4 oz) dark chocolate together in a bowl over gently simmering water. When melted, stir in 75 g (3 oz) icing sugar. Take off the heat and add 100 g (4 oz) of thick, whipped cream. Leave in the fridge until the mixture begins to thicken. Spread over one cake and place the other cake on top.

If you want to make this as a pudding, try putting the mixture in six individual ramekin dishes or in a well greased spring form tin 25.5-cm (10-inch) and bake until risen and slightly moist in the middle (see photograph opposite).

Fattening, irresistible and definitely sheer heaven!

Loxton's Amazing Cake

'SOPHIE'S CHOICE' CHOCOLATE MOUSSE CAKE

Sophie is a great friend of ours and is one of those brilliant 'effortless' cooks who makes entertaining round the kitchen table take on a new meaning. This recipe was left to her as a 'thank you' present by a happy guest.

Makes one 25-cm (10-inch) cake

4 eggs, separated
equal weight of caster sugar
equal weight of butter

equal weight of unsweetened plain chocolate
1 tablespoon self-raising flour

Line a 25-cm (10-inch) diameter spring form cake tin with greased foil. Place the egg yolks in a bowl with the sugar. Beat until thick and pale.

Melt the butter in a heavy-based pan with the chocolate. Add to the creamed egg mixture, mixing well. Fold in the flour.

Whisk the egg whites until they stand in stiff peaks. Fold into the chocolate mixture. Spoon into the prepared cake tin and bake in a preheated oven, 180°C/350°F (gas mark 4), for about 45 minutes, or until well risen and springy.

Cool in the tin.

These are our very favourite CHOCOLATE CHIP COOKIES: Cream together 225 g (8 oz) butter with 175 g (6 oz) soft brown sugar and 175 g (6 oz) caster sugar until soft. Gradually add 2 beaten eggs, then stir in 1 teaspoon of vanilla essence. Gently stir in 250 g (9 oz) self-raising flour, 1 teaspoon bicarbonate of soda, 1 teaspoon of baking powder and 1 teaspoon of salt. Add 345 g (12 oz) chocolate chips. Spoon teaspoonfuls of the mixture on to greased baking trays, keeping them quite small and spaced well apart because the mixture will spread during cooking. Bake in a moderate oven, 180°C/350°F (gas mark 4) for 10 to 12 minutes. Makes about 40 delicious cookies.

Sarah

CHOCOLATE BROWNIES

Makes about 12 brownies

75 g (3 oz) butter
75 g (3 oz) dark chocolate
225 g (8 oz) granulated sugar
1 tablespoon chocolate powder
2 large eggs
25 g (1 oz) ground almonds
75 g (3 oz) self-raising flour
100 g (4 oz) pecan nuts,
crushed

Melt the butter and dark chocolate together in a bowl over gently simmering water. Stir well. Add the sugar and chocolate powder and stir really well. Beat the eggs in a separate bowl and mix into the chocolate mixture. Fold in the ground almonds, flour and pecan nuts. Pour into a greased 18- x 28-cm (7- x 11-inch) tin.

Bake in the centre of a preheated oven, 180°C/350°F (gas mark 4), for about 20 minutes. The timing can vary so I suggest you test after 20 minutes. The brownies should still be sticky in the middle when prodded with a skewer, but firm to the touch.

Cool slightly and cut in squares.

DOUBLE CHOCOLATE HAZELNUT BROWNIES

Makes about 16 brownies

75 g (3 oz) butter, softened
50 g (2 oz) bitter or
unsweetened chocolate
225 g (8 oz) caster sugar
2 eggs, beaten
½ teaspoon vanilla essence
75 g (3 oz) plain flour
50 g (2 oz) toasted hazelnuts,
chopped
50 g (2 oz) chocolate chips

Be warned – these are extremely more-ish! They are also useful to keep in the freezer as an emergency pudding.

Melt the butter and chocolate over a low heat. Remove from the heat and add the sugar, eggs and vanilla essence, mixing together well. Fold in the flour and spoon into a greased 20-cm (8-inch) square cake tin. Sprinkle with the hazelnuts and chocolate chips, pressing them lightly into the top of the brownie mixture.

Bake in a preheated oven, 180°C/350°F (gas mark 4), for about 30-35 minutes. Cool then cut into squares.

My daughter India is allergic to hazelnuts, so I just double the quantity of chocolate chips.

Sarah

PEANUT BUTTER COOKIES

Makes about 30 cookies

350 g (12 oz) butter
100 g (4 oz) soft light brown
sugar
150 g (5 oz) granulated sugar
175 g (6 oz) crunchy peanut
butter
1 egg, beaten
150 g (5 oz) plain flour
½ teaspoon baking powder
½ teaspoon vanilla essence

Cream the butter with the sugars and peanut butter until light and fluffy. Beat in the egg, mixing well. Sift the flour with the baking powder and fold into the creamed mixture with the vanilla essence. Shape into a long roll about 4 cm (1½ inches) in diameter. Wrap in clingfilm and chill until firm.

Unwrap the cookie mixture and slice thinly into about 30 rounds. Place well apart on lightly greased baking trays. Bake in a preheated oven, 180°C/350°F (gas mark 4), for 12-15 minutes, or until crisp and golden.

Cool on a wire rack. They keep well if they get the chance.

COCONUT BISCUITS

Makes about 14 biscuits

100 g (4 oz) butter
100 g (4 oz) shredded coconut
50 g (2 oz) dark brown sugar
50 g (2 oz) muscovado sugar
100 g (4 oz) ground rice
50 g (2 oz) corn flour

This recipe really couldn't be simpler! Mix all the ingredients together. Divide the dough and roll into about 20 walnut-sized balls.

Place well apart on two lightly greased baking trays and flatten slightly with a fork.

Bake in a preheated oven, 180°C/350°F (gas mark 4), for about 12 minutes, until brown and crisp.

PISTACHIO COOKIES

Makes about 20

100 g (4 oz) butter
100 g (4 oz) light brown sugar
1 egg
100 g (4 oz) plain flour
½ teaspoon vanilla essence
75 g (3 oz) pistachio nuts,
chopped

Cream the butter with the sugar. Beat in the egg until well mixed. Fold in the flour, then add the vanilla essence and pistachio nuts, stirring well.

Place small mounds of the mixture (about the size of a dessertspoon) on greased baking trays, spacing well apart. Bake in a preheated oven, 190°C/375°F (gas mark 5) for about 12 minutes, or until pale brown and cooked. Cool on a wire rack.

LUMPY BISCUITS

Makes about 20 biscuits

100 g (4 oz) plain flour
½ teaspoon baking powder
100 g (4 oz) butter
175 g (6 oz) soft dark brown
sugar
50 g (2 oz) caster sugar
1 egg, beaten
1 tablespoon natural yoghurt
100 g (4 oz) jumbo oats

This is a recipe from my childhood. My mother made them when I had friends for tea. They're still my favourite and everyone always likes them. They are mis-shapen, so they really do look home-made.

Sift the flour with the baking powder. Cream the butter with the sugars until pale and fluffy. Beat in the egg and yoghurt, mixing well. Add the flour, half at a time, then fold in the oats, mixing well.

Drop tablespoonfuls of the mixture onto greased baking trays (well apart because they spread) and bake in a preheated oven, 180°C/350°F (gas mark 4), for 12-14 minutes, or until pale brown and cooked.

Cool on a wire rack.

I make these biscuit recipes but I refrigerate the dough and slice off and bake as many biscuits as I need at any one time. The dough will keep in the refrigerator for 3-4 days if wrapped in clingfilm or foil — they taste doubly delicious if baked fresh daily.

Sarah

NO-NONSENSE LEMON AND RICE CAKE

A plain cake with a great taste – it can be sliced and buttered but I think it's best left alone.

Makes one 15-cm (6-inch) square cake

100 g (4 oz) butter
200 g (7 oz) caster sugar
grated rind of 2 lemons
2 egg yolks

175 g (6 oz) self-raising flour
50 g (2 oz) ground rice
juice of 1 lemon

Line a 15-cm (6-inch) square cake tin with greaseproof paper.

Cream the butter with the sugar and lemon rind until light and fluffy. Beat in the egg yolks with 4 tablespoons of the flour. Fold in the remaining flour with the ground rice and lemon juice.

Spoon into the prepared tin and bake in a preheated oven, 180°C/350°F (gas mark 4), for 60-70 minutes, or until a skewer inserted comes out clean. Cool in the tin then turn out.

GILLIAN'S LEMON LOAF is so good that you must try it — now! Sift 250 g (9 oz) plain flour with ½ teaspoon salt and 1½ teaspoons baking powder. Stir in 350 g (12 oz) caster sugar. Place this mixture and 175 g (6 oz) butter in a food processor and whirl to mix. Add 3 beaten eggs, 175 ml (6 fl oz) milk and whirl quickly to just mix (don't overmix). Pour into a lightly greased 900-g (2-lb) loaf tin and bake in a preheated oven, 180°C/350°F (gas mark 4), for 1¼ hours. Allow to cool for 10 minutes then turn out onto a cooling rack and brush with this glaze: Bring 6 tablespoons lemon juice and 25 g (1 oz) sugar to the boil and cook for 3 minutes. Brush over the cake.

CELEBRATION CAKE

I made both my daughter's wedding cakes. I made them from this recipe (one of my mother's handed down in turn from her mother). This quantity makes a 25-cm (10-inch) deep round cake, so if you were making a wedding cake you would have to work out the sizes (and number of cakes) needed and adjust the recipe accordingly. Sarah's cake was two-tiered with the top covered in violets and trailing violet ribbons. Emma's was three-tiered – each tier resting on the one below. At the base and between each tier I arranged masses of gypsophila, and on the top more gypsophila with champagne-coloured roses and again trailing ribbons. This is a very effective way of making a cake look beautiful – real flowers, some leaves and lots of ribbons – and forget all those stereotyped decorations. I make the cake for birthdays and Christmas and it's always a success. Try it – you won't be disappointed.

Makes one 25-cm (10-inch) round cake

350 g (12 oz) plain flour
2 teaspoons ground mixed spice
1 teaspoon freshly ground black pepper
1 teaspoon ground cinnamon
1.25 kg (2 ½ lb) mixed dried fruit (use chopped dates, figs, apricots, sultanas etc. – whichever is your favourite combination)
225 g (8 oz) glacé fruit (use whole glacé fruit and chop it yourself rather than the ready-chopped

red and green variety)
100 g (4 oz) pecans, chopped
50 g (2 oz) flaked almonds
grated rind of 1 orange
grated rind of 1 lemon
275 g (10 oz) butter
275 g (10 oz) caster sugar
8 eggs
small wineglass of rum or brandy

Line a 25-cm (10-inch) round cake tin with greaseproof paper.

Sift the flour with the mixed spice, black pepper and cinnamon. Add the mixed fruit, glacé fruit, walnuts, almonds and orange and lemon rinds.

Cream the butter with the sugar until pale and fluffy. Beat in the eggs, one at a time. Fold in the dry ingredients and rum or brandy.

Spoon into the prepared cake tin. Bake in a preheated oven, 120°C/250°F (gas mark ½), for 3-4 hours, or until a skewer inserted into the centre of the cake comes out clean. Allow to cool slightly in the tin then turn out onto a wire rack to cool. Store wrapped in foil in an airtight tin for several weeks to mature.

SIMPLE SUPPERS

Eating in the evening is a movable feast – an informal
dinner party, early meal with the children, late night supper or
merely something on a tray while watching the latest soap
on television. Whatever or wherever it is, here are
some suggestions.

Nanette

BLACK BEAN SOUP

Serves 6-8

1.25 kg (2½ lb) black beans, soaked overnight in
cold water
1.2 litres (2 pints) chicken or
vegetable stock
1.2 litres (2 pints) water
100 g (4 oz) lean back bacon, rinded
1 ham bone
25 g (1 oz) unsalted butter
1 onion, peeled and chopped

1 carrot, peeled and chopped
2 small leeks, chopped
50 g (2 oz) celery tops, chopped
small bunch of fresh parsley
pinch of dried thyme
1 bay leaf
freshly ground black pepper
salt
soured cream to serve

Rinse and drain the beans in cold water and put them in a large pan. Add the stock, water, bacon and ham bone. Bring to the boil, reduce the heat and simmer while preparing the vegetables.

Melt the butter in a pan, add the onion, carrot, leeks, celery tops and parsley. Cook, over a gentle heat, until softened. Add to the soup with the thyme, bay leaf and pepper to taste. Cover and simmer until the beans are very soft and tender, stirring occasionally. This will take about 3 hours.

Remove the bacon, bay leaf and ham bone. Thin the soup with extra stock if liked (personally, I find the texture perfect). Taste and adjust the seasoning with salt and pepper.

Serve the soup piping hot with a spoonful of soured cream.

When I make this soup, I make sure I have a stack of warmed tortillas to eat with it. They make an interesting change from bread.

Sarah

ANGELA'S ABSOLUTELY EVERYTHING SOUP

This is a recipe that I have stolen from my friend Angela. It's absolutely delicious and very filling – a meal in itself.

Serves 6-8

225 g (8 oz) red kidney beans or haricot beans
100 g (4 oz) salt pork, diced
2 cloves of garlic, peeled and finely chopped
1 Spanish onion, peeled and quartered
4 carrots, peeled and finely sliced
4 sticks of celery, finely chopped
1.2 litres (2 pints) of chicken or
vegetable stock
½ small head of cabbage, coarsely shredded
4 leaves of curly endive, coarsely shredded

4 tomatoes, skinned and coarsely chopped
225 g (8 oz) green beans, topped and tailed and
coarsely chopped
100 g (4 oz) frozen peas
100 g (4 oz) short-cut macaroni
salt
freshly ground black pepper
2 tablespoons chopped fresh parsley
2 tablespoons olive oil
4 tablespoons freshly grated Parmesan cheese

Cook the beans in boiling salted water until tender, about 2 hours. Drain and set aside.

Dry-fry the salt pork in a heavy-based frying pan until golden. Add the garlic and onion and cook until softened. Transfer to a large saucepan, stir in the carrot, celery and stock. Bring to the boil, reduce the heat and simmer for 10 minutes.

Add the cabbage, endive, tomatoes, green beans and cooked beans.

Bring to the boil, reduce the heat, cover and simmer for 1½ hours until really tender.

Stir in the frozen peas and macaroni with salt and pepper to taste. Bring to the boil, reduce the heat and simmer until the macaroni is tender, about 15 minutes. Stir in the parsley and olive oil.

Serve hot sprinkled with the freshly grated Parmesan cheese and with chunks of interesting bread.

NO-BEEF BURGERS

I don't like my children eating red meat, so I invented these burgers for a birthday party treat. I managed to kill quite a few birds with one stone with this recipe because you can cram hidden vegetables and fibre into them – grown-ups also fight for the leftovers! Serve them with miniature wholewheat buns, a little mayonnaise and ketchup and children will forget that McDonald's ever existed!

Serves 6 children or 4 adults

700 g (1½ lb) lean chicken or turkey, minced
2 carrots, peeled and grated
2 courgettes, trimmed and grated
¼ onion, peeled and grated
2 tablespoons chopped fresh parsley
3 tablespoons tomato ketchup

1 tablespoon bran or wheatgerm
3 tablespoons oatmeal
salt
freshly ground black pepper
4-6 tablespoons dried breadcrumbs
2 tablespoons sunflower oil

Mix the chicken or turkey with the carrots, courgettes, onion, parsley, tomato ketchup, bran or wheatgerm, oatmeal and salt and pepper. Divide and shape into about 12 small patties.

Coat in the breadcrumbs and chill for 15 minutes.

To cook, heat the oil in a large frying pan and sauté the chicken burgers until golden and crisp, about 3-4 minutes on each side. Drain on absorbent paper.

Serve hot in miniature wholewheat buns, topped with a little mayonnaise and tomato ketchup.

Although if one's honest, nothing beats french fries with burgers, but should you want to break with tradition, your children will love these SHOCKING PINK POTATOES: Make mashed potatoes in the usual way with lashings of butter and milk and add a couple of puréed cooked beetroot.

Sarah

LAYERED SHEPHERD'S PIE

When Sarah and I were living at home we always looked forward to the weekends. The house would be full of family and friends and the kitchen was like Waterloo Station. We were given jobs and, as we became more reliable, allowed to invent and cook our own dishes. I'm sure some of them must have been awful but we were always encouraged. My mother used to say there was method in her madness, since she knew one day we would become good cooks and she and my father would be coming to our homes for dinner. I'm glad to say that happens a lot. This is something I often serve.

Serves 4

2 teaspoons vegetable oil
1 onion, peeled and chopped
700 g (1½ lb) lean minced beef, lamb or chicken
400 g (14 oz) can peeled plum tomatoes, coarsely chopped
1 teaspoon yeast extract
1 stock cube, crumbled
salt

freshly ground black pepper
300 g (10 oz) packet of frozen creamed spinach
450 g (1 lb) carrots, peeled and sliced
1 tablespoon double cream
450 g (1 lb) peeled potatoes
15 g (½ oz) butter
1-2 tablespoons milk
50 g (2 oz) Cheddar cheese, grated

Heat the oil in a pan, add the onion and sauté until softened. Stir in the meat and cook until well browned and no longer pink. Add the tomatoes, yeast extract, stock cube and salt and pepper. Bring to the boil, reduce the heat, cover and simmer for 30 minutes or thereabouts.

Cook the spinach according to the packet instructions and set aside. Cook the carrots in boiling salted water until tender. Drain and mash with the cream and salt and pepper.

Cook the potatoes in boiling salted water until tender. Drain and mash with the butter and milk until creamy.

Place the meat mixture in the base of a large deep ovenproof dish. Top with the spinach. Cover with the carrot and finally top with the potatoes. Sprinkle with the grated cheese.

Bake in a preheated oven, 200°C/400°F (gas mark 6), for about 30-40 minutes, or until the top has crisped up and turned pale brown.

Layered Shepherd's Pie

MAGGIE'S MEAT LOAF

Maggie is a great friend. She is a great cook and here is her GREAT meat loaf.

Serves 8

3 egg yolks
3 tablespoons water
25 g (1 oz) porridge oats
1.4 kg (3 lb) lean minced beef or lamb
2 carrots, peeled and grated
1 large onion, peeled and finely chopped
1 clove of garlic, peeled and crushed (optional)
3 tablespoons tomato ketchup
2 tablespoons wholegrain French mustard
2 tablespoons chopped fresh parsley
2 tablespoons chopped fresh mixed herbs
(for example, rosemary, thyme, sage, chives
and chervil)

2 teaspoons lemon juice
pinch of chilli powder
2 teaspoons salt
1 teaspoon freshly ground black pepper
227 g (8 oz) can chilli sauce or

HOME-MADE TOMATO TOPPING:
227 g (8 oz) can tomatoes, drained and chopped
2 tablespoons tomato purée
2 tablespoons soft brown sugar
1 tablespoon cider vinegar
1 tablespoon made mustard
2 tablespoons chopped fresh parsley

Stir the egg yolks with the water and oats and leave to stand for 10 minutes.

Mix the beef or lamb with the carrots, onion, garlic, if used, tomato ketchup, mustard, parsley, herbs, lemon juice, oat mixture, chilli powder and salt and pepper. Place on a very slightly greased baking tray and shape into a loaf. Top with the chilli sauce or Home-made Tomato Topping.

To prepare the tomato topping by mixing the ingredients in a small pan. Bring to the boil, reduce the heat and simmer until thick and pulpy, about 10-15 minutes.

Bake in a preheated oven, 180°C/350°F (gas mark 4), for 1½ hours until cooked.

Serve hot with creamy whipped potatoes and steamed sprouting broccoli, or cold with salad.

If you have any of this left over, it is wonderful to have sliced in sandwiches the next day. Add pickle, lettuce, mayonnaise or whatever you want.

Nanette

FOUR SEASONS VEGETABLE BAKE

Serves 4-6

225 g (8 oz) long-grain brown
rice
1 vegetable stock cube
250 ml (8 fl oz) hot water
about 1 kg (2 lb) prepared
fresh vegetables
100 g (4 oz) mature Cheddar
cheese, grated
salt
freshly ground black pepper
25 g (1 oz) butter

This is a dish that I make when all of my favourite vegetables are in season. It is delicious enough to eat on its own.

Cook the rice in boiling salted water, according to the packet instructions, until tender, about 30 minutes. Drain thoroughly. Dissolve the stock cube in the hot water and set aside.

Meanwhile, steam the vegetables until just tender but still crisp. Mix with the rice and place in a large shallow ovenproof dish. Moisten with the stock. Sprinkle with the cheese, season to taste with salt and pepper and dot with the butter.

Bake in a preheated oven, 180°C/350°F (gas mark 4), for 15-20 minutes until the cheese has melted and the rice and vegetable mixture is hot.

BULGUR PILAF WITH PINE NUTS

Serves 4

1 large onion, finely chopped
2 tablespoons butter
finely grated rind of 1 lemon
finely grated rind of 1 orange
225 g (8 oz) bulgur wheat
300 ml (½ pint) chicken stock
50 g (2 oz) raisins
50 g (2 oz) pine nuts, lightly
toasted
8 spring onions, finely chopped
chopped parsley

Cook the onion in the butter. Add the lemon and orange rind and the bulgur wheat and stir gently to mix. Gradually add the stock. Stir in the raisins and bring to the boil.

Put the lid on, reduce the heat and simmer gently for about 10 minutes or until the bulgur wheat has absorbed most of the stock.

Fluff up the bulgur wheat with a fork and stir in the pine nuts, parsley and spring onions.

Serve when cooled.

TURKEY AND PUMPKIN PIE

Why not try this on Thanksgiving Day?

Serves 6

12 baby button onions, peeled
450 ml (¾ pint) water
2 tablespoons cornflour
150 ml (¼ pint) milk
75 g (3 oz) Cheddar cheese
salt
freshly ground black pepper

450 g (1 lb) cooked turkey, chopped
350 g (12 oz) slice of pumpkin, peeled, seeded
and cubed
2 tablespoons chopped fresh parsley
250 g (8¾ oz) packet frozen puff pastry, thawed
beaten egg to glaze

Cook the onions in the water until just tender, about 8-10 minutes. Mix the cornflour with the milk and blend into the onion mixture. Bring to the boil, stirring constantly, until smooth and thick. Add the cheese and salt and pepper. Fold in the turkey, pumpkin and parsley. Spoon into a 1.2-litre (2-pint) pie dish.

Roll out the pastry to an oval or round about 4 cm (1½ inches) larger than the pie dish. Trim a 2.5-cm (1-inch) strip from the edge of the pastry to make a pastry collar. Moisten the pie dish rim with water and press the pastry collar firmly on to the rim, overlapping the ends. Dampen the pastry collar with water then top with the pastry lid and press firmly together. Trim away any excess pastry and knock up the crust to seal. Flute the edges of the pie and decorate with any pastry trimmings. Glaze with beaten egg. Bake in a preheated oven, 220°C/425°F (gas mark 7), for about 25-30 minutes, or until the pastry is well-risen and golden and the filling is piping hot.

Serve at once with jacket potatoes and a green vegetable.

Turkey and Pumpkin Pie

FRIDAY FISH PIE

Serves 4

900 g (2 lb) haddock
salt
freshly ground white pepper
1 bay leaf
150 ml (¼ pint) water
40 g (1½ oz) butter
25 g (1 oz) flour
150 ml (¼ pint) milk
100 g (4 oz) frozen peas
2 tablespoons chopped fresh parsley

1 tablespoon chopped fresh tarragon
pinch of ground nutmeg
100 g (4 oz) peeled prawns
2 tablespoons double cream

TOPPING:
50 g (2 oz) butter
75 g (3 oz) fresh breadcrumbs
25 g (1 oz) hazelnuts, chopped
50 g (2 oz) Cheddar cheese, grated

Place the fish fillets in a buttered ovenproof dish and season with salt and pepper. Add the bay leaf and water, cover with foil and bake in a preheated oven, 160°C/325°F (gas mark 3), for 15 minutes or until the fish is tender. Skin and flake the fish, reserving all the cooking juices.

Melt the butter in a pan. Add the flour, blending well and cook for 1 minute. Gradually add the milk and 150 ml (¼ pint) of the reserved cooking juices, stirring well. Bring to the boil, stirring constantly, and cook until smooth and thickened. Remove from the heat and add the peas, parsley, tarragon, nutmeg and salt and pepper. Fold in the prawns, flaked fish and cream. Spoon into a medium buttered pie or gratin dish.

To make the topping, melt the butter in a heavy-based frying pan. Add the breadcrumbs and stir around until golden. Remove from the heat, stir in the hazelnuts and cheese. Sprinkle over the fish mixture. Cook under a preheated hot grill until bubbly, about 2 minutes.

Serve at once with grilled or oven-baked tomato halves.

TROUT KEDGEREE

This is a simple dish and very quick to make if you have all the ingredients ready beforehand.

Serves 4

225 g (8 oz) long-grain rice
50 g (2 oz) butter
1 bunch of spring onions, trimmed and chopped
225 g (8 oz) smoked trout, boned and flaked
3 hard-boiled eggs, shelled and chopped

1 bunch of baby spinach, finely chopped
salt
freshly ground black pepper
3 tablespoons double cream
2 tablespoons toasted flaked almonds

Cook the rice in boiling salted water until tender. Drain thoroughly.

Melt the butter in a large shallow pan, add the spring onions and sauté until tender, about 5 minutes (do not allow to brown). Mix in the rice and trout and cook until hot. Add the eggs, baby spinach and salt and pepper. Stir in the cream and almonds and cook for 1-2 minutes until hot. Serve at once.

You could try this with kippers instead of trout for a special occasion breakfast.

BAKED TROUT WITH VEGETABLE SAUCE: Place two trout in an ovenproof dish. Put a few knobs of butter inside each fish with a little lemon juice and salt and pepper. Melt 25 g (1 oz) butter in a small pan and blend in a small glass of white wine and the juice of 1 lemon. Pour this over the trout and bake for about 25 minutes in a medium oven. To make the vegetable sauce, whizz together a bunch of spring onions, 1 small red pepper and 3 skinned, medium tomatoes and add to the trout for the last 5 minutes of cooking time.

Nanette

SEAFOOD SUPPER

Every summer we take the children to Cornwall and this is really the perfect meal for the end of a bucket-and-spade-filled day. Sometimes the children manage to catch a few shrimps, but they'll never part with them for this recipe.

Serves 4

1 tablespoon sunflower oil
1 onion, peeled and finely chopped
½ green pepper, cored, seeded and sliced
½ red pepper, cored, seeded and sliced
225 g (8 oz) long-grain brown rice
large pinch of turmeric or powdered saffron
600-900 ml (1-1½ pints) fish stock

550 g (1¼ lb) mixed cooked shelled shellfish (for example, prawns, shrimps, crab, lobster, mussels, clams or oysters)
salt
freshly ground black pepper
2 tablespoons chopped fresh parsley

Heat the oil in a large shallow pan. Add the onion and sauté until softened. Stir in the peppers, rice and turmeric or saffron and cook for 2 minutes, stirring constantly.

Add sufficient stock to cover the rice mixture. Cover and simmer for 25 minutes, stirring occasionally, pour in a little more stock if the mixture begins to cook dry.

Stir in the prepared shellfish and season with salt and freshly ground black pepper. Cover and cook for a further 5 minutes or until the shellfish are thoroughly heated through and the rice is cooked and all the stock has been absorbed. Stir in the parsley and serve.

Why not finish the meal with Cornish ice cream in a cone.

Seafood Supper

Nanette

SPAGHETTI WITH UNCOOKED FRESH TOMATO SAUCE

Some of the best recipes are the simplest. This is from Mariella, who lives in Rome; it is a spaghetti to serve in the summer. The tomatoes must be very ripe, and of course the spaghetti must be cooked al dente.

Serves 3

4 very large ripe tomatoes, skinned and very finely chopped
5 tablespoons good-quality olive oil
juice of 1 lemon

3 tablespoons chopped fresh basil
salt
freshly ground black pepper
250 g (9 oz) spaghetti

At least 4 hours before required, mix the tomatoes with 4 tablespoons of the oil, the lemon juice, basil and salt and pepper. Leave to stand, covered, until ready to serve.

Bring a large pan of water to the boil and add the remaining olive oil and the spaghetti. Boil briskly, uncovered, for 8-10 minutes (or according to the packet instructions), until the pasta is cooked *al dente*. Drain thoroughly and place in a large warmed serving dish.

Add the prepared fresh tomato sauce and toss lightly.

Serve at once with a salad of fresh green lettuce hearts.

One of the best and quickest pasta sauces I know (quantities can vary depending on what you have available): Chop about 8 tomatoes, add torn basil, pepper and salt, chopped spring onions, dash of olive oil and a dash of balsamic vinegar. Mix in a small tub of ricotta cheese. Mix with hot pasta (I like penne) and top with shavings of Parmesan. Serve immediately.

Nanette

MACARONI CHEESE WITH MUSHROOMS

I have made this more times than I care to remember – but Graham loves it and never seems to mind.

Serves 4

1 tablespoon olive oil
350 g (12 oz) macaroni
50 g (2 oz) butter
25 g (1 oz) plain flour
600 ml (1 pint) milk
100 g (4 oz) Cheddar or Red Leicester
cheese, grated

225 g (8 oz) cooked ham, chopped
100 g (4 oz) button mushrooms, cooked
salt
freshly ground black pepper
3 tomatoes, sliced
2 tablespoons freshly grated Parmesan cheese

Bring a large pan of water to the boil and add the olive oil and the macaroni. Boil briskly, uncovered, for 8-10 minutes (or according to the packet instructions), until the pasta is cooked *al dente*. Drain thoroughly and set aside.

Melt the butter in a pan. Add the flour, blending well and cook for about 1 minute.

Gradually add the milk, bring to the boil, stirring constantly, and cook until thickened. Remove from the heat and stir in the cheese, ham, mushrooms and salt and pepper.

Place the macaroni in a medium ovenproof dish and pour over the sauce, making sure that it covers all of the pasta. Top with the sliced tomatoes and sprinkle with the Parmesan cheese.

Bake in a preheated oven, 200°C/400°F (gas mark 6), for about 20-25 minutes until the cheese is brown and bubbly.

Serve hot with a green salad.

FIRST IMPRESSIONS

Some people behave as though there was an unwritten law that states you must always serve a 'first course'. That's rubbish.

It may suit you, or your guests, to just have a main course followed by fruit and cheese, or a starter followed by a pudding. That's why we've selected first courses that can be juggled around.

They can create your first course impression for a three course dinner party or be adjusted to become a main feature – it all depends on you.

Nanette

PUMPKIN SOUP

Serves 6

450 g (1 lb) fresh pumpkin,
peeled and cut into small cubes
2 large potatoes, peeled and
chopped
900 ml (1½ pints) chicken
stock
750 ml (1¼ pints) milk
½ teaspoon ground nutmeg
½ teaspoon ground ginger
1 teaspoon salt
freshly ground black pepper
6 tablespoons soured cream

*This is wonderful as a first course. When we lived in America,
I liked to serve it before a traditional Thanksgiving feast.*

Boil the pumpkin in lightly salted water until tender,
about 45 minutes. Drain and set aside. Boil the
potatoes in lightly salted water until tender, about 15-20
minutes. Drain and set aside.

Place the pumpkin, potatoes and about half of the
chicken stock in a blender or food processor and purée
until smooth.

Place in a large saucepan and add the remaining stock,
milk, nutmeg, ginger and salt and pepper to taste, mixing
well. Bring to the boil, reduce the heat and simmer for 5
minutes. Serve hot in soup bowls topped with a spoonful
of soured cream.

CHILLED PINK SOUP

Serves 6

15 g (½ oz) butter
2 onions, peeled and chopped
2 carrots, peeled and grated
6 (medium) cooked beetroot,
skinned and grated
1.8 litres (3 pints) chicken
stock
2 teaspoons sugar
juice of 1 lemon
salt
freshly ground black pepper
1 teaspoon creamed
horseradish
450 ml (¾ pint) soured cream
chopped fresh dill

*This soup is lovely just as it is. I serve it with chunks of black
bread. You can pass around a bowl of croûtons and finely
chopped spring onions.*

Melt the butter in a large pan. Add the onions and
carrots and cook for about 10 minutes but don't let
them brown. Add the beetroot, stock and sugar and
simmer for 30 minutes.

Mix in the lemon juice, salt and pepper to taste and
horseradish. Cool then purée in a blender or food
processor until smooth. Chill thoroughly.

Stir the soured cream into the soup and ladle into
chilled soup bowls.

RED PEPPER SOUP

Serves 6

15 g (½ oz) butter
1 tablespoon olive oil
6 medium red peppers, cored,
seeded and cut into pieces
1 large onion, chopped
1 medium potato, peeled and
cut into pieces
1 clove of garlic, chopped
1.8 litres (3 pints) chicken
stock
1 bay leaf
salt
freshly ground black pepper
250 ml (8 fl oz) buttermilk or
single cream

When my husband was appearing in Noel Coward's Tonight
at 8.30, *one of the acts was called 'Red Peppers'. For a first
night party I made this, but it's so good that I've been cooking it
ever since. You can serve it hot or cold.*

Heat together the butter and oil in a large pan. Add
the peppers, onion, potato and garlic. Cover and
cook, over a moderate heat, until tender but not brown,
stirring whenever you think about it.

Add the chicken stock, bay leaf and salt and pepper.
Bring to the boil, reduce the heat, cover and simmer for
45-50 minutes, or until all the vegetables are tender.
Remove and discard the bay leaf.

Purée in a blender or food processor until smooth. Stir
in the buttermilk or single cream and adjust the seasoning
if necessary. Serve hot or chilled.

WATERCRESS SOUP

Serves 4

50 g (2 oz) butter
450 g (1 lb) leeks, sliced
450 g (1 lb) potatoes, chopped
900 ml (1½ pints) chicken or
vegetable stock
salt
freshly ground black pepper
2 bunches of watercress,
trimmed
150 ml (¼ pint) double cream

Melt the butter in a large pan. Add the leeks and
potatoes and cook for about 5 minutes, stirring
constantly. Add the stock and salt and pepper to taste and
bring to the boil. Reduce the heat, cover and simmer for
15 minutes, or until the vegetables are tender. Add the
watercress and purée the soup in a blender or food
processor until smooth.

Stir in the cream just before serving. This soup is also
great served chilled.

Watercress Soup,
American Corn Bread (page 26)

CARROT AND PEAR SOUP

Serves 4

25 g (1 oz) butter
450 g (1 lb) carrots, peeled and sliced
6 spring onions, sliced
2 ripe pears, peeled, cored and chopped
450 ml (¾ pint) chicken stock
grated rind and juice of

1 orange
salt
freshly ground black pepper
150 ml (¼ pint) crème fraîche
chopped fresh mint

Melt the butter in a large pan. Add the carrots and spring onions and cook for about 5 minutes but do not allow to brown. Stir in the pears and cook for another 5 minutes. Add the chicken stock, orange rind, orange juice and salt and black pepper.

Bring to the boil, reduce the heat, cover and simmer until the carrots are tender. Cool slightly.

Purée in a blender or food processor. Chill thoroughly. Just before serving stir the cream into the chilled soup. Serve sprinkled with the chopped mint.

CHILLED TOMATO SOUP: Tomato soup always sounds very ordinary but when it's home made it tastes anything but. Purée 1.25kg (2½ lb) very ripe, skinned tomatoes in a blender then sieve to remove any pips. Blend in gradually 2 tablespoons cornflour. Heat gently, stirring until thickened. Remove from the heat, stir in 1 tablespoon of sugar, 1 teaspoon onion juice, grated rind and juice of 1 lemon, and salt and pepper to taste. Chill thoroughly. Just before serving, stir in 150 ml (½ pint) double cream and sprinkle with some chopped basil.

Nanette

— *Nanette* —

PEPPER AND ANCHOVY HORS D'OEUVRES

Serves 4

2 red peppers, cored, seeded
and sliced
2 green peppers, cored, seeded
and sliced
few drops of vinegar
50 g (2 oz) can anchovies,
drained
15 g (½ oz) butter
4 teaspoons walnut oil
150 ml (¼ pint) double cream

This is an unusual starter that tastes much better than it reads. I first had it in a little Italian restaurant and they let me have the recipe.

Cook the peppers in boiling water with a few drops of vinegar, until just tender. Drain and reserve the liquid.

Purée the anchovies or (better still) pound to a smooth paste with a pestle and mortar. Heat the butter and oil in a pan, add the anchovies and cook gently for 1 minute over a low heat. Add the cream and stir until thickened but don't let it boil.

Place the peppers in a heated serving dish. Pour over the anchovy cream to coat then serve at once with chunks of toasted wholemeal bread.

— *Emma* —

SMOKED FISH PÂTÉ

Serves 4-6

4 smoked mackerel fillets,
skinned and boned
100 g (4 oz) cream cheese
2 tablespoons horseradish
relish
juice of 1 lemon (or even more
if you like a lemony taste)
50 g (2 oz) butter, melted
150 ml (¼ pint) double cream
freshly ground black pepper

This is so easy to make. It's delicious served as a starter with brown toast, or as a dip with raw carrot and celery strips.

Put everything in a blender or food processor and purée until smooth. Add pepper to taste, mixing well.
Spoon into a serving dish and chill.

I make this as well — but I use smoked trout instead of mackerel and I leave out the cream using 1 tablespoon of mayonnaise instead.

Nanette

TUNA MOUSSE

Serves 6-8

I sometimes make this mousse in individual moulds – turn them out then gently wrap in a slice of smoked salmon.

439 g (15½ oz) can tuna, drained
300 ml (½ pint) mayonnaise
1 heaped dessertspoon creamed horseradish
300 ml (½ pint) double cream, whipped
2 tablespoons chopped fresh parsley
1 tablespoon chopped fresh dill
1 tablespoon lemon juice

salt
freshly ground black pepper
15 g (½ oz) powdered gelatine
4 tablespoons water
2 egg whites
¼ cucumber, sliced
chopped fresh dill

Purée the tuna, 2 tablespoons of the mayonnaise and the horseradish in a blender or food processor until smooth. Add the cream, remaining mayonnaise, parsley, dill, lemon juice and salt and pepper to taste, mixing well.

Dissolve the gelatine in the water and stir into the tuna mixture. Whisk the egg whites until they stand in stiff peaks. Fold into the tuna mixture. Pour into a lightly oiled 1.25-litre (2¼ pint) ring mould, cover and chill until set – about 2 hours.

To serve, dip briefly into hot water and invert onto a serving plate. Serve surrounded with cucumber slices and sprinkled with sprigs of fresh dill.

I occasionally make this as a main course and fill the centre of the ring with prawns.

Emma

Tuna Mousse

CHEESE AND HERB SOUFFLÉS

Serves 4

25 g (1 oz) butter
25 g (1 oz) plain flour
300 ml (½ pint) milk
4 eggs, separated
1 egg white
50 g (2 oz) Cheddar cheese, grated
50 g (2 oz) freshly grated Parmesan cheese
salt
freshly ground black pepper
3 tablespoons chopped fresh herbs

Fresh Parmesan cheese is so much nicer than the ready-grated sort.

People are always impressed by soufflés – and yet they really couldn't be easier to make. Just make sure everyone has been seated a few minutes before you take them out of the oven.

Prepare 4 small soufflé or ovenproof soup bowls by buttering lightly then coating with a little Parmesan cheese or breadcrumbs.

Melt the butter in a pan. Add the flour and cook for 1 minute. Gradually add the milk, bring to the boil, stirring until smooth and thickened. Remove from the heat and stir in the egg yolks, one at a time, mixing well. Add the cheeses, salt and pepper and the herbs.

Whisk the egg whites until they stand in stiff peaks. Stir 1 tablespoon into the cheese mixture then fold in the remainder. Divide between the prepared bowls and bake in a preheated oven, 180°C/350°F (gas mark 4), for about 20 minutes, or until puffed-up and pale brown on top (keep your eyes on them).

To serve, place each soufflé dish on a napkin in the centre of a large dinner plate. Serve at once, of course.

AVOCADOS BAKED WITH BRIE

Serves 4

2 avocados, halved and stoned
1 tablespoon lemon juice
about 175 g (6 oz) Brie, thinly sliced

This is quick and easy – that's why I like it.

Brush the cut surface of each avocado with the lemon juice. Fill the hollows with sliced Brie. Cook under a preheated hot grill until the Brie is bubbly. Serve at once.

FRIED BRIE WITH RASPBERRY PURÉE

Serves 4

about 350-400 g (12-14 oz)
wedge **Brie** cheese, not too ripe
50 g (2 oz) plain wholewheat
flour
2 eggs, beaten
175 g (6 oz) wholewheat
breadcrumbs
25 g (1 oz) flaked almonds,
coarsely chopped
450 g (1 lb) frozen raspberries
6 tablespoons water
50 g (2 oz) sugar
oil for deep frying

Remove the rind from the Brie and cut into 12 pieces about the size of a walnut. Dust with the flour, dip in the beaten egg and roll in the breadcrumbs and almonds to coat. Chill for at least 2 hours for the coating to become firm before cooking.

Meanwhile, to make the sauce, place the raspberries, water and sugar in a heavy-based pan and cook until pulpy, for about 10 minutes. Cool slightly then sieve to remove the seeds.

Heat the oil in a deep-fat fryer or pan to about 190°C/375°F, or until a cube of bread will brown. Add the Brie pieces and deep-fry until crisp and golden. Drain well on absorbent paper.

Reheat the raspberry purée until hot. Place the Brie pieces on a warmed serving plate and surround with the warm raspberry purée. They are delicious with French or other crisp, interesting bread.

PEAR AND STILTON SALAD

Serves 4

3 tablespoons walnut oil
1 tablespoon wine vinegar
½ teaspoon Dijon mustard
salt
freshly ground black pepper
2 bunches of watercress
4 ripe pears, peeled, cored and
thinly sliced
175 g (6 oz) Stilton cheese
4 tablespoons chopped walnuts

Beat the oil with the vinegar, mustard and salt and pepper to taste. Arrange the watercress in the centre of four dinner plates then arrange the pears attractively on top. Pour the dressing over the pears. Crumble the cheese and sprinkle over the pears, with the walnuts.

Serve with oatmeal crackers.

MANGO WITH SMOKED CHICKEN

Serves 4

2 large ripe mangoes, sliced
1 tablespoon lemon juice
100 g (4 oz) cream cheese
2 tablespoons crème fraîche
2 tablespoons crushed roasted hazelnuts
100 g (4 oz) smoked chicken, finely chopped
salt

freshly ground black pepper
a selection of salad leaves

DRESSING:
2 tablespoons hazelnut oil
2 teaspoons wine vinegar
pinch of finely grated lemon rind

Arrange the mango slices on a salad leaf lined plate and drizzle with the lemon juice.

Beat the cream cheese with the crème fraîche, hazelnuts, chicken and salt and pepper until well mixed.

Spoon the mixture on to the plates next to the mango slices.

To make the dressing, beat the oil with the vinegar, lemon rind and salt and pepper to taste. Drizzle over the salad leaves just before serving.

Short on time, then chop watermelon into cubes and place in chilled glasses. Sprinkle with vodka and serve. Sounds odd but tastes delicious!

Nanette

CUCUMBER AND GRAPE JELLY

Serves 4-6

125 g (4 ¾ oz) packed lime-
flavoured jelly
1 small cucumber, peeled and
thinly sliced
salt
freshly ground white pepper
100 g (4 oz) seedless white
grapes, halved
lemon slices

The perfect starter for hot summer days.

Dissolve the jelly in hot water to make up to 450 ml (¾ pint) and let it cool until syrupy but not set.

Put the cucumber slices between sheets of absorbent paper and press them to remove excess water.

Season the jelly with salt and pepper. Add the cucumber and grapes and mix. Spoon into a serving dish or decorative mould and chill to set (preferably overnight or for 4-6 hours).

Serve with lemon slices. You could try serving this with more thinly sliced cucumber, tossed in a favourite vinaigrette dressing.

MINTED CUCUMBER AND TOMATO SALAD

Serves 4

½ cucumber, cut into thin strips
2 small tomatoes, sliced
4 carrots, peeled and grated
3 courgettes, grated

DRESSING:
2 tablespoons sunflower oil
3 tablespoons mint sauce
1 teaspoon French mustard
1 teaspoon clear honey
salt
freshly ground black pepper

This is a fresh-tasting salad to serve as a starter or as a side dish with pasta.

Put the cucumber in a serving bowl with the tomatoes, courgettes and carrots. To make the dressing, beat the oil with the mint sauce, mustard, honey and salt and pepper to taste. Pour over the salad and toss. Cover and chill for about 1 hour before serving.

GRAPEFRUIT SORBET

Serves 4

300 ml (½ pint) water
150 g (5 oz) sugar
150 ml (¼ pint) fresh
grapefruit juice (pink
grapefruit is nice)
1 egg white

Place the water and sugar in a heavy-based pan. Heat slowly to dissolve the sugar then boil for about 6 minutes. Add the grapefruit juice (strained if necessary), mixing well, and leave to cool.

Pour into a shallow freezer tray and freeze until mushy (about 1 hour).

Transfer the grapefruit mixture to a bowl and whisk until smooth. Whisk the egg white until it stands in stiff peaks. Fold into the grapefruit mixture. Return to the freezer tray, cover, seal and freeze until firm or spoon into scooped-out grapefruit shells and freeze until firm.

About 30 minutes before serving, put the sorbet in the refrigerator to soften. Spoon into chilled glasses or set the fruit shells on individual serving plates. Serve at once.

TOMATO SORBET

Serves 4-6

4 very large ripe tomatoes,
skinned
2 drops of Tabasco or 2
teaspoons Worcestershire sauce
juice of ½ lemon
salt
freshly ground black pepper
1 egg white
fresh mint sprigs
1 lemon, sliced, optional

Cut the tomatoes in half and squeeze over a fine sieve to remove the seeds, keeping the strained juice. Chop the tomatoes and put in a blender or food processor with the tomato juice, Tabasco or Worcestershire sauce, lemon juice and salt and pepper. Purée until smooth, pour into a shallow freezer tray and freeze until mushy (about 1 hour).

Whirl in the blender or food processor or beat with a whisk until smooth. Whisk the egg white until it stands in stiff peaks. Fold into the tomato mixture. Return to the freezer tray, cover, seal and freeze until firm.

About 30 minutes before serving, remove the sorbet from the freezer to the refrigerator to soften. Spoon into chilled wine glasses and serve garnished with fresh mint and lemon slices if wished. Serve at once.

Tomato Sorbet

THE MAIN EVENT

If you are giving a dinner party the menu usually slots into place once you have decided upon the main course. You can make the principal course your star turn and forget about starters or puddings. Serve something with drinks before dinner and offer fruit and cheese at the end. Whichever way you choose to organise your dinners, here are some of our collective ideas.

Nanette

STRIPED FISH TERRINE

Serves 4

225 g (8 oz) haddock fillets, skinned
50 g (2 oz) fresh white breadcrumbs
1 tablespoon milk
2 eggs, beaten
1 tablespoon fromage frais
1 tablespoon double cream
2 tablespoons chopped fresh parsley

1 tablespoon chopped fresh chives
pinch of ground nutmeg
pinch of cayenne pepper
salt
freshly ground black pepper
450 g (1 lb) spinach leaves
2-4 scallops (depending upon size)

Put the haddock fillets in a blender or food processor and process until finely chopped. Soak the breadcrumbs in the milk, add to the fish with the eggs, fromage frais, cream, parsley, chives, nutmeg, cayenne pepper and salt and pepper. Purée until smooth.

Trim, sort and wash the spinach leaves. Place in a pan with just the water clinging to the leaves. Cook until limp, squeeze to remove any excess water then chop very finely. Stir in the fish mixture, mixing well. Trim and discard the black vein from the scallops. Separate the white flesh from the coral flesh. Thinly slice the white flesh horizontally. Line a 900-ml (1½-pint)

terrine with greased foil. Place half of the haddock mixture in the base of the terrine and cover with the white and coral scallop flesh, pressing down firmly. Top with the remaining fish mixture, cover tightly with greased foil and place in a bain-marie or roasting pan half-filled with boiling water. Cook in a preheated oven, 180°C/350°F (gas mark 4), for 1 hour.

Remove the terrine from the bain-marie and leave to cool. Unmould onto a serving plate, cover and chill thoroughly.

This terrine is very good with home-made tomato sauce or home-made mayonnaise flavoured sharply with lemon.

GINGERED SALMON EN CRÔUTE

Serves 8

1.25 kg (2½ lb) salmon tailpiece
100 g (4 oz) butter
3 tablespoons raisins
3 tablespoons blanched almonds, coarsely chopped
4 pieces preserved ginger, chopped
10 cooked asparagus spears
salt
freshly ground black pepper
450 g (1 lb) shortcrust pastry
beaten egg to glaze

HERB AND LEMON SAUCE:
50 g (2 oz) butter
2 shallots, peeled and finely chopped
1 teaspoon finely chopped fresh chervil
1 teaspoon finely chopped fresh tarragon
1 teaspoon finely chopped fresh parsley
1 teaspoon plain flour
300 ml (½ pint) single cream
1 teaspoon Dijon mustard
2 egg yolks
juice of 1 lemon

Ask the fishmonger to skin and bone the salmon into two fillets. Mix the butter with the raisins, almonds and ginger. Spread half of this filling over one of the salmon fillets and top with the asparagus spears. Season generously with salt and pepper. Cover with the second fish fillet and remaining butter mixture.

Roll out the pastry thinly and cut out two long oval shapes. Place the fish sandwich on top of one of the pastry pieces, set on a lightly greased baking tray. Cover with the second pastry piece and press the edges together firmly to seal. Trim and flute or crimp the edges attractively. Roll out the pastry trimmings and cut into small fish shapes. Glaze the pastry with beaten egg, place the decorative fish shapes in position and glaze again. Make a few deep slashes in the top of the pastry crust to allow any steam to escape.

Bake in a preheated oven, 220°C/ 425°F (gas mark 7), for 30-35 minutes, until the fish is cooked and the pastry is crisp and golden.

Meanwhile, to make the sauce, melt the butter in a pan. Add the shallots, chervil, tarragon and parsley and cook until softened. Stir in the flour and then all but 2 tablespoons of the cream. Add the mustard and salt and pepper to taste. Simmer gently for 10 minutes. Mix the egg yolks with the reserved cream and stir into the sauce. Cook over a gentle heat until the sauce thickens – don't allow to boil. Add the lemon juice just before serving.

To serve, transfer the salmon to a warmed serving plate, surround with a selection of cooked vegetables. Serve with the hot Herb and Lemon Sauce.

Gingered Salmon en Croûte

LEMON SOLE STUFFED WITH SMOKED SALMON AND SPINACH

Serves 2

1 large lemon sole
100 g (4 oz) cooked chopped
spinach
2 tablespoons cream cheese
pinch of ground nutmeg
salt
freshly ground black pepper
2 very thin slices smoked
salmon
juice of 1 lemon
40 g (1½ oz) butter, melted
fresh tarragon leaves

This is a very special, very simple dish to serve two people, but it's easy to prepare for many more.

Ask the fishmonger to skin and fillet the sole to give you two fillets. Mix the spinach with the cheese, nutmeg and salt and pepper. Place a slice of smoked salmon on each lemon sole fillet. Divide the stuffing evenly and spread over the fish. Roll the fillet up loosely to enclose the filling and secure with wooden cocktail sticks.

Place in a buttered ovenproof dish and squeeze over the lemon juice. Brush with the melted butter and scatter over a few fresh tarragon leaves. Cook in a preheated oven, 180°C/350°F (gas mark 4), for 15 minutes.

Serve hot with tiny new potatoes and mangetout.

LEMON COD

Serves 4

4 cod steaks
juice of 2 lemons
2 tablespoons green or pink
peppercorns
50 g (2 oz) butter
fresh dill
freshly ground black pepper

This fish is easy on the pocket and the waistline.

Place each cod steak on a piece of foil large enough to enclose the fish. Squeeze over the lemon juice and peppercorns. Dot with the butter and top with a few sprigs of fresh dill and pepper to taste. Fold and secure into a parcel shape.

Bake in a preheated oven, 180°C/350°F (gas mark 4), for 20 minutes, or until the fish is cooked and flakes easily with a fork. Serve piping hot in the foil envelopes with jacket-baked potatoes.

FETTUCINE WITH SMOKED SALMON AND FRESH PEAS

Serves 8

3 tablespoons olive oil
700 g (1½ lb) fettucine verdi
150 g (5 oz) shelled fresh peas or mangetout, trimmed
100 g (4 oz) thinly sliced smoked salmon

600 ml (1 pint) double cream
1 tablespoon chopped shallot
2 tablespoons dry white wine
salt
freshly ground black pepper

Bring a large pan of water to the boil and add 1 tablespoon of the olive oil and the pasta. Boil briskly, uncovered, for 4-6 minutes (or according to the packet instructions), until the pasta is cooked *al dente*. Drain thoroughly, add the remaining olive oil and toss lightly to coat. Set to one side and keep warm.

Meanwhile, blanch the peas or mangetout for 2 minutes, drain and plunge into iced water. Place half of the smoked salmon in a blender or food processor with 2 tablespoons of the double cream and the shallot. Purée until smooth. Cut the remaining smoked salmon into thin strips. Place the wine in a heavy-based pan and bring to the boil. Add the remaining cream and cook, stirring constantly, until the mixture thickens and will coat the back of a spoon. Add the salmon purée, mixing well. Season to taste with salt and black pepper.

Stir the peas or mangetout, salmon strips and hot sauce into the pasta. Toss lightly, spoon into a warmed serving dish and serve at once.

ROZ'S SIMPLE FISH CAKES

My friend Roz gave me this fish cake recipe. These are so simple to make, but taste heavenly. You can use smoked haddock and fresh haddock mixed (which Roz says is her favourite), or cod, or salmon or, at a pinch, tuna.

Poach 450 g (1 lb) fish with about 300 ml (½ pint) milk, and then flake but not too finely. Boil 450 g (1 lb) potatoes, then mash with a little butter and milk. Mix the fish and potato mixtures together, with an egg and some parsley, vinegar, salt and pepper. Divide and shape into patties — how many depends on your appetite! Coat each patty in flour. Dip the patties into a beaten egg then in fresh breadcrumbs to coat. Chill thoroughly to firm for about 1 hour before cooking. To cook, fry until golden and crisp on all sides. Drain on absorbent paper. Roz serves these with an egg sauce. I serve them on a bed of creamed spinach.

Nanette

CRABCAKES

This recipe is from a favourite restaurant in Beverly Hills. It's the most popular dish on the menu.

Makes 4-6

450 g (1 lb) crabmeat
juice of 1 lemon
25 g (1 oz) butter
75 g (3 oz) plain flour
10 tablespoons milk
½ teaspoon mustard powder
2 egg yolks
4 teaspoons capers, coarsely chopped
cayenne pepper

salt
freshly ground white pepper
1 egg
75 g (3 oz) fresh white breadcrumbs
25 g (1 oz) unsalted butter
2 tablespoons sunflower oil
lemon wedges
mayonnaise to serve

Mash the crabmeat with the lemon juice. Melt the butter in a pan. Add one-third of the flour and cook for about 1 minute.

Gradually add 6 tablespoons of the milk and bring to the boil, stirring constantly, until you have a smooth and really thick white sauce.

Remove from the heat, stir in the mustard, egg yolks, capers, cayenne pepper and salt and white pepper to taste, mixing well. Stir in the crabmeat mixture and mix until all the ingredients are combined.

Cover and chill for at least 1 hour. Divide and shape the crabmeat mixture into 4-6 patties. Coat the remaining flour. Beat the egg with the remaining milk. Dip the patties into the milk mixture then in the breadcrumbs to coat. Chill thoroughly to firm for about 1 hour before cooking. To cook, heat together the unsalted butter and the oil in a large frying pan. Add the crabcakes and sauté until golden and crisp on all sides. Drain on absorbent paper.

Serve hot with huge wedges of lemon and lashings of mayonnaise.

Crabcakes, The Best Potato Salad (page 125)

QUICK CHICKEN WITH MINT

Serves 6

Quick, easy and delicious – the perfect summer evening dish.

6 chicken breasts, skinned
chicken stock

DRESSING:
3 tablespoons safflower oil
3 tablespoons walnut oil
2 tablespoons white wine
vinegar
1½ teaspoons Dijon mustard
½ teaspoon sugar
salt
freshly ground black pepper
very large bunch of fresh mint,
chopped

Poach the chicken breasts in sufficient chicken stock to cover until tender, about 10 minutes. Cover and leave to cool in the stock. When cool, remove from the stock and slice into thin strips.

To make the dressing, beat the oils with the vinegar, mustard, sugar and salt and pepper. Stir in the mint and pour over the chicken. Cover and leave to marinate for 1 hour.

To serve, arrange the chicken strips in a fan shape on a serving dish. Serve with tiny new potatoes and a crisp green salad.

The chicken may be served on individual dishes – the chicken slices arranged to alternate with slices of avocado and strips of cucumber. Serve with hot Granary bread.

Sarah

DRESSED-UP CHICKEN

Serves 4

4 boneless chicken breasts,
skinned
25 g (1 oz) plain flour
2 eggs, beaten
50 g (2 oz) Granary
breadcrumbs
4 slices smoked ham
4 slices Mozzarella cheese
salt
freshly ground black pepper

Coat the chicken breasts in the flour. Dip into the beaten egg and coat in the breadcrumbs. Chill for about 20 minutes.

Place on a baking tray and cook in a preheated oven, 190°C/375°F (gas mark 5), for 30-40 minutes, or until the chicken is cooked (when pierced any juices will run clear). Remove from the oven, cover each chicken breast with a slice of ham and a slice of cheese. Season with salt and pepper, return to the oven and cook for a further 8-10 minutes, or until the cheese is bubbly and melted. Serve on a bed of fresh baby spinach with a spoonful of your favourite chutney.

CHICKEN BAKED WITH HONEY, COURGETTE AND TOMATO

This is very easy to make and has a light, subtle flavour. It's great served with a mixed salad or baked potatoes topped with soured cream and chives.

Serves 4

4 chicken breasts, skinned
25 g (1 oz) plain flour
3 tablespoons sunflower oil
½ small onion, peeled and finely chopped
1 clove of garlic, peeled and crushed

6 medium courgettes, chopped
400 g (14 oz) can chopped tomatoes
salt
freshly ground black pepper
2 tablespoons clear honey

Lightly coat the chicken breasts in the flour. Heat 2 tablespoons of the oil in a frying pan. Add the chicken breasts and sauté until browned on all sides. Remove from the pan and place in a flameproof casserole dish.

Heat the remaining oil in a pan. Add the onion, garlic and courgettes and cook, over a moderate heat, until the onion is softened. Add the tomatoes and salt and pepper to taste and stir around.

Spread the honey over the chicken breasts, then pour over the tomato mixture. Cover and bake in a preheated oven, 180°C/ 350°F (gas mark 4), for 30 minutes. Remove from the oven and cook, uncovered, under a preheated hot grill until crisp and golden. Serve at once.

HERB CHICKEN WITH ORANGE AND BASIL SAUCE

This is the perfect make-ahead cold chicken dish – the chicken rolls can be made the day before required, the sauce can be whipped up just before it's needed, and a green salad and crusty bread are all you need to go with it.

Serves 4

4 boneless chicken breasts, skinned
225 g (8 oz) fresh white breadcrumbs, lightly toasted
½ onion, peeled and finely chopped
1 clove of garlic, peeled and crushed
40 g (1½ oz) chopped fresh herbs
2 eggs, beaten
salt
freshly ground black pepper

ORANGE AND BASIL SAUCE:
6 tablespoons olive oil
4 tablespoons orange juice
2 tablespoons lemon juice
grated rind of ½ orange
1 clove of garlic, peeled and crushed
2 tablespoons chopped fresh basil
mayonnaise

Place the chicken breasts between sheets of greaseproof paper and beat until flat.

Mix the breadcrumbs with the onion, garlic, herbs, beaten egg and salt and pepper to taste. Spread the stuffing over the rough side of the chicken breasts and roll up to enclose. Secure with wooden cocktail sticks. Place, seam-side down, on a lightly greased baking dish. Cover with greaseproof paper and bake in a preheated oven, 190°C/375°F (gas mark 5), for 20-30 minutes, or until the chicken is cooked. Allow to cool.

To make the sauce, mix the oil with the orange juice, lemon juice, orange rind, garlic and basil. Add sufficient mayonnaise to the mixture to make a sauce that resembles a runny hollandaise.

Cut the stuffed chicken breasts diagonally into thin slices and arrange in a fan on a serving plate.

Drizzle over the sauce to serve.

CHICKEN AND RED ONION PIE

You can really get carried away decorating this dish with pastry shapes. Why not cut out your guests' initials, hearts or leaves – or whatever takes your fancy.

Serves 6

50 g (2 oz) butter
2 red onions, peeled and chopped
100 g (4 oz) button mushrooms, wiped and sliced
50 g (2 oz) plain flour
300 ml (½ pint) chicken stock
150 ml (¼ pint) dry white wine
25 g (1 oz) eating apple, chopped
675 g (1½ lb) cooked chicken, thinly sliced

50 g (2 oz) cooked dried apricots, thinly sliced
1 tablespoon chopped fresh parsley
salt
freshly ground black pepper
370 g (13 oz) packet frozen puff pastry, thawed
beaten egg to glaze
2 teaspoons sesame seeds

Melt the butter in a pan. Add the onions and sauté until soft. Add the mushrooms and cook briefly. Stir in the flour and cook for 1 minute. Gradually add the chicken stock and wine. Stir in the apple, bring to the boil and stir until lightly thickened. Remove from the heat, fold in the chicken, apricots, parsley and salt and pepper. Spoon into a 1.5-litre (2½-pint) pie dish.

Roll out the pastry to a round or oval about 2.5 cm (1 inch) larger than the dish. Cut a narrow strip from around the pastry and use to cover the dampened rim of the dish. Brush the pastry rim with water and cover with the pastry lid. Seal the edges firmly, trim and crimp attractively.

Decorate with cut-out pastry shapes. Make a hole in the crust to allow any steam to escape. Glaze with beaten egg and sprinkle with the sesame seeds.

Bake in a preheated oven, 200°C/400°F (gas mark 6), for 25-30 minutes, or until the pastry is well risen, cooked and golden brown.

Serve with seasonal vegetables.

CHICKEN IN SOURED CREAM WITH RED PEPPERS AND AVOCADO

This is a good dish to prepare for larger buffet-style dinner parties.

Serves 4-6

6 boneless chicken breasts
chicken stock
1 red pepper, cored, seeded and sliced
150 ml (¼ pint) soured cream
2 tablespoons mayonnaise

2 tablespoons chopped fresh chives
salt
freshly ground black pepper
1 ripe avocado, peeled, stoned and sliced

Poach the chicken breasts in sufficient chicken stock to cover until tender, about 10 minutes. Cover and leave to cool in the stock. When cool, remove from the stock and slice into thin strips. Mix the chicken with the pepper. Blend the soured cream with the mayonnaise, chives and salt and pepper to taste. Fold into the chicken mixture with the avocado slices.

I like to serve this on a bed of lettuce with cooked French beans drizzled with vinaigrette dressing.

STIR-FRIED DUCK WITH GINGER

Serves 4

3 tablespoons sunflower oil
2.5-cm (1-inch) piece root ginger, peeled
4 duck breasts, skinned and cut into strips
225 g (8 oz) bean sprouts
227 g (8 oz can) waterchestnuts, drained and
sliced
½ red pepper, cored, seeded and sliced
½ yellow pepper, cored, seeded and sliced
2 spring onions, trimmed and chopped
soy sauce
1 tablespoon dry sherry

Heat the oil in a wok or large frying pan. Add the ginger and cook for 1 minute. Remove it with a slotted spoon and reserve the oil.

Cut the piece of ginger in half and chop one half finely (use the other half for another recipe).

Add the duck strips to the very hot oil and stir-fry, tossing constantly, until just cooked. Add the bean sprouts, waterchestnuts, peppers, spring onions, the chopped reserved ginger, soy sauce to taste and sherry. Stir-fry for 1-2 minutes until very hot. Serve at once.

Why not try serving this with GINGERED VEGETABLES (page 133), but leave out the ginger!

GLAZED TARRAGON TURKEY

Serves 4

4 small unboned turkey breasts
salt
freshly ground black pepper
25 g (1 oz) butter

2 tablespoons finely chopped shallot
2 tablespoons finely chopped fresh tarragon
6 tablespoons dry white wine
3 tablespoons water

Season the turkey with salt and pepper. Melt the butter in a large frying pan, add the turkey breasts, skin-side down, and sauté until golden, about 10 minutes. Turn over and cook, over a gentle heat, for a further 5 minutes. Remove the turkey from the pan with a slotted spoon and set aside.

Add the shallot to the pan juices and cook until softened. Stir in the tarragon, wine and water. Return the turkey breasts to the pan, skin-side up. Cover and cook, over a low heat, for 15 minutes.

Remove the cover and continue to cook, adding a little more wine if necessary, for a further 5 minutes, basting the turkey frequently with the juices, under tender and evenly glazed. Serve with a green vegetable.

I often use baby new potatoes, baked in a little olive oil with rosemary and crushed garlic.

Sarah

PASTA WITH DOLCELATTE CHEESE AND HAM

This is one of my favourite dinner party dishes as it is incredibly easy to prepare.

Serves 6

1 tablespoon olive oil
500 g (18 oz) dried pasta shells or bows
600 ml (1 pint) double cream
450 g (1 lb) Dolcelatte cheese, crumbled

225 g (8 oz) lean ham, finely sliced
freshly ground black pepper
chopped fresh parsley

Bring a large pan of water to the boil and add the olive oil and pasta. Boil briskly, uncovered, for 10-12 minutes (or according to the packet instructions), until the pasta is cooked *al dente*. Drain the pasta thoroughly. Spoon into a warmed serving dish and keep warm. Meanwhile, place the cream and cheese in the top of a double boiler or in a bowl over simmering water and cook until the cheese melts (don't take your eyes off it!). Add the ham and pepper to taste, stirring well to mix.

Pour over the cooked pasta and toss gently to coat.

Serve at once sprinkled with plenty of chopped fresh parsley.

BAKED HAM IN APPLE JUICE

Serves about 8

2-2.5 kg (4½-5 lb) joint smoked middle gammon,
soaked overnight
apple juice
Demerara sugar

ORANGE AND LEMON SAUCE:
grated rind and juice of 1 lemon
juice of 3 oranges
2 tablespoons redcurrant jelly
1 tablespoon made mustard
1 tablespoon vinegar
1 tablespoon creamed horseradish

Place the gammon in a large pan and cover with apple juice. Bring to the boil, reduce the heat and simmer gently for three-quarters of the calculated cooking time, allowing 25 minutes per 450 g (1 lb). Drain, reserving the cooking juices.

Remove the outer skin and score the fat attractively in a diamond pattern with a sharp knife. Sprinkle with Demerara sugar and press into the skin. Place in a roasting tin with a little of the reserved apple juice.

Bake in a preheated oven, 160°C/325°F (gas mark 3), for the remaining quarter of the cooking time.

Meanwhile, to make the sauce, mix the lemon rind with the lemon and orange juices, redcurrant jelly, mustard, vinegar and horseradish. Heat gently until everything is well blended.

Serve warm with the hot sliced ham. The nice thing about this recipe is that the ham and sauce are equally good cold.

Baked Ham in Apple Juice

PORK CASSEROLE

Serves 4

900 g (2 lb) pork shoulder, trimmed and cut into
chunky cubes
2 tablespoons groundnut oil
25 g (1 oz) butter
20 shallots, peeled and left whole
2 cooking apples, peeled and sliced

600 ml (1 pint) cider
150 ml (¼ pint) cider vinegar
bunch fresh thyme
2 bay leaves
salt
freshly ground black pepper

Sauté the pork in half of the oil and butter until browned. Remove the pork from the pan and set aside. Sauté the shallots and apple in the pan using the remaining oil and butter. Add the cider and cider vinegar and mix together. Return the meat to the pan, add the herbs and season with the salt and pepper. Simmer gently for about 2 minutes.

Transfer everything to a casserole dish (don't put the lid on) and cook in a preheated oven, 180°C/350°F (gas mark 4) for approximately 2 ¼ hours, stirring occasionally. Serve with mashed potatoes.

LAMB WITH HARICOT BEANS

Serves 6

2.75 kg (6 lb) leg of lamb
50 g (2 oz) butter
6 large cloves of garlic, peeled
½ teaspoon cloves

HARICOT BEAN ACCOMPANIMENT:
450 g (1 lb) haricot beans
chicken stock or water to cover
50 g (2 oz) butter
1 large carrot, sliced
1 stick celery, finely chopped
1 large onion, chopped
1 bouquet garni
pinch of dried cloves
chopped fresh parsley
glass of wine or port

Soak the haricot beans overnight, drain and rinse. In 25 g (1 oz) butter, soften the carrot, celery and onion. Add the beans, and just enough water or chicken stock to cover. Add a pinch of dried cloves and the bouquet garni. Simmer for 2 hours, until beans are tender. (This can be prepared in advance.)

Purée 225 g (8 oz) of the bean mixture in a blender. Stir this into the rest of beans, add the remaining butter and a handful of chopped parsley. Stir and serve with the lamb when ready.

Smear the lamb with 50 g (2 oz) butter and spike with the garlic and cloves. Cook the lamb for 15 minutes, in a preheated oven, 230°C/450°F (gas mark 8). Reduce the oven temperature to 180°C/350°F (gas mark 4), and cook for a further 2 ½ hours, basting occasionally with the juices.

During the last 30 minutes of cooking, pour over the glass of wine or port.

Lamb simply roasted with a sprinkling of juniper berries, garlic and plenty of rosemary is hard to beat.

Nanette

BRAMLEY CROWN OF LAMB

Serves 4-6

4 teaspoons sunflower oil
1 small onion, peeled and chopped
1 stick of celery, chopped
50 g (2 oz) carrots, peeled and chopped
25 g (1 oz) sultanas
225 g (8 oz) Bramley apples, peeled, cored and
chopped
50 g (2 oz) cooked long-grain rice

2 tablespoons chopped fresh parsley
lemon juice
salt
freshly ground black pepper
1 crown roast of lamb (with a total of 14 cutlets)
apple wedges
watercress sprigs

Heat the 3 teaspoons of the oil in a pan. Add the onion and celery and sauté until just soft. Add the carrots, sultanas and apples and cook for 3-5 minutes, stirring continously. Add the rice and parsley then sharpen with lemon juice. Season with salt and pepper.

Place the crown roast in a greased roasting tin and fill the centre with the stuffing mixture, pressing down firmly.

Cover the stuffing and bone ends with foil to prevent charring. Brush with the remaining oil and roast in a preheated oven, 190°C/375°F (gas mark 5), for 1¼ -2 hours, according to taste.

Serve hot decorated with apple wedges and watercress, and with your favourite seasonal vegetables.

Bramley Crown of Lamb

CALF'S LIVER WITH ROSEMARY

Serves 4

50 g (2 oz) butter
1 tablespoon grated onion
4 large thin slices calf's liver
2 tablespoons chopped fresh rosemary

salt
freshly ground black pepper
2 tablespoons dry sherry or light meat stock
fresh rosemary sprigs

Melt the butter in a heavy-based frying pan. Add the onion and sauté. Add the liver and sprinkle with half of the rosemary and salt and pepper. Cook gently for 3 minutes until golden on the underside. Turn over, sprinkle with the remaining rosemary and salt and pepper. Cook for a further 2 minutes or until done.

Remove from the pan and arrange on a warmed serving dish.

Stir the sherry or stock into the pan juices. Cook for 1 minute to reduce slightly then pour over the cooked liver. Put a few rosemary sprigs on top of the liver and serve with lemon wedges to squeeze over.

Delicious with steamed mangetout.

TABLE IDEAS

Recently I bought 12 small inkwells in a junk shop. They are blue glass and about 8 centimetres high. They look great on a dining table, placed among candles with either one small flower in each or some lily of the valley or snowdrops.

If you ever buy water that comes in blue bottles, don't throw the empty bottle out. Soak off the label and put six in a line like soldiers down the centre of a long table, and place one long-stemmed white rose in each.

Fill a large bowl (or basket) with apples and decorate with leaves.

Place a single rose in a small vase in front of each guest.

Fill a bowl or basket with lots of African violets left in their pots, then tie trailing purple ribbons around your candlesticks.

Scoop out the insides of globe artichokes and place a night light in the centre of each.

Put unusual flowers in jam jars, then tie a napkin around like a collar.

Try arranging a large basket of raw vegetables with herbs and flowers for the centre of the table — you can then eat your table centrepiece with a dip as a first course.

Collect lots of large fir cones, pile into a basket, add holly and walnuts. Decorate with red velvet bows and you have a Christmas table centrepiece that even the children can make.

SIDE ORDERS

When vegetables are young and fresh, you can't beat just steaming them with nothing more elaborate than perhaps a sprinkling of herbs. However, when they are not at their peak, they need a bit of dressing up – here are some ways of doing it.

Nanette

BAKED SWEET POTATOES WITH CHIVES

Serves 4-6

450 g (1 lb) sweet potatoes or
yams, scrubbed
1 tablespoon butter
4 tablespoons soured cream
2 tablespoons chopped fresh
chives

Rub the sweet potatoes or yam skins with the butter. Bake in a preheated oven, 220°C/425°F (gas mark 7), for 30 minutes. Prick the skins with a fork and continue to bake until tender.

Remove from the oven, split and gently squeeze up the flesh. Place in a warmed serving dish. Top with the soured cream mixed with the chives.

Serve hot.

THE BEST POTATO SALAD

Serves 6

8 slices streaky bacon, rinded
900 g (2 lb) small new potatoes
6 spring onions, trimmed and
chopped
3 tablespoons chopped fresh
mint
1 stick of celery, chopped
2 tablespoons soured cream
2 tablespoons mayonnaise
salt
freshly ground black pepper
1 Iceberg lettuce, shredded
fresh mint sprigs to decorate

Potato salad can be very boring – this one isn't!

Grill the bacon until very crisp, drain on absorbent paper then crumble.

Cook the potatoes in their skins in boiling salted water until tender, about 12-15 minutes. Drain and cool.

Place the potatoes in a bowl with the spring onions, bacon, mint and celery. Mix the soured cream with the mayonnaise and season with salt and pepper. Add to the potato mixture and toss lightly.

Spoon into a serving bowl lined with the chopped lettuce.

Decorate with mint sprigs to serve.

RED CABBAGE WITH MARROW AND PRUNES

Serves 4-6

900 g (2 lb) red cabbage,
coarsely shredded or grated
50 g (2 oz) butter
225 g (8 oz) marrow, peeled
and sliced (with seeds)
100 g (4 oz) pitted prunes,
chopped
3 tablespoons lemon juice
250 ml (8 fl oz) apple juice
1 tablespoon soft brown sugar
salt
freshly ground black pepper

Blanch the cabbage in boiling salted water for 2-3 minutes. Drain thoroughly.

Melt the butter in a pan. Add the marrow and sauté until softened. Stir in the cabbage, prunes, lemon juice, apple juice, sugar and salt and pepper.

Spoon into a medium casserole dish, cover and cook in a preheated oven, 180°C/350°F (gas mark 4), for 45-60 minutes, stirring half-way through the cooking time.

Serve hot.

SAUTÉED RADISHES

Serves 2-4

15 g (½ oz) butter
1 large bunch of radishes,
trimmed and sliced
2 tablespoons soured cream
1 teaspoon coarse sea salt

Melt the butter in a pan. Add the radishes and cook until just tender, about 8 minutes, stirring occasionally.

Drain away any excess juices, stir in the soured cream and sprinkle with sea salt.

Serve at once.

BRAISED FENNEL ITALIAN-STYLE

Serves 4

2 heads of fennel
50 g (2 oz) butter, melted
3 tablespoons freshly grated Parmesan cheese
1 clove of garlic, peeled and crushed
salt
freshly ground black pepper
2 tomatoes, skinned and chopped
2 rashers back bacon, rinded and chopped
chopped fresh parsley

Trim the stems and outer leaves off the fennel, reserving the frilly leaves. Cut each fennel head into three equal slices. Cook in boiling water for 2 minutes, then drain thoroughly. Coat the fennel slices in the melted butter and arrange in a shallow ovenproof dish. Sprinkle with the Parmesan cheese, garlic and salt and pepper. Cover with the chopped tomatoes and bacon.

Bake, uncovered, in a preheated oven, 180°C/350°F (gas mark 4), for 20-25 minutes or until the fennel is tender and the topping is crisp and browned. Sprinkle with chopped parsley and decorate with the reserved frilly fennel leaves.

Serve hot with grilled meat or fish.

STEAMED CARROTS WITH FENNEL AND HAZELNUTS

Serves 4

450 g (1 lb) young baby carrots, trimmed
25 g (1 oz) butter
1 tablespoon chopped fresh fennel
25 g (1 oz) hazelnuts, toasted and chopped

Steam the carrots until tender, about 10-15 minutes depending upon size and maturity. Toss in the butter, fennel and hazelnuts.

Spoon into a warmed serving dish.

Emma

GREEK STUFFED TOMATOES

This is a light meal in itself or a tasty vegetable accompaniment. The inspiration for the recipe came during a holiday in Greece where baked stuffed tomatoes are served in countless ways – this is my favourite.

Serves 4

4 very large Beef tomatoes
8 tablespoons cooked long-grain rice
salt
freshly ground black pepper
1 tablespoon sunflower oil
1 clove of garlic, peeled and crushed

150 g (5 oz) cucumber, peeled and chopped
150 g (5 oz) mushrooms, sliced
1 teaspoon cornflour
50 g (2 oz) crumbled Feta cheese
fresh parsley sprigs

Lightly grease an ovenproof dish. Cut the tops off the tomatoes and carefully scoop out the flesh using a teaspoon. Leave the tomato shells to drain, upside-down, on absorbent paper for a few minutes.

Chop the flesh of two of the tomatoes and place in a bowl with the cucumber, rice and salt and pepper (using the remaining flesh for another dish). Heat the oil in a small pan, add the garlic and mushrooms and sauté but don't let the garlic brown. Stir in the cornflour, blending well. Add to the rice mixture and mix thoroughly. Spoon the mixture into the tomato shells and place in the dish. Sprinkle with the cheese and replace the tomato lids.

Bake in a preheated oven, 190°C/375°F (gas mark 5), for 15-20 minutes.

Serve at once sprinkled with parsley.

STUFFED PEPPERS: Cut a pepper (any colour) in half. Mix together some crushed garlic, basil, anchovies, cherry tomatoes and black olives with salt and pepper. Pile into the pepper and drizzle over a little olive oil. Bake in a medium oven for at least one hour. Serve warm or cold with ciabatta.

Nanette

HERBED RATATOUILLE

Serves 4-6

2 medium aubergines, cubed
salt
5 tablespoons olive oil
2 large onions, sliced
2 red peppers, cored, seeded
and sliced
4 courgettes, sliced
2 cloves of garlic, crushed
1 teaspoon ground coriander
3 large tomatoes, skinned
and chopped
freshly ground black pepper
2 tablespoons chopped basil

Place the aubergines in a colander or sieve and sprinkle with salt. Leave to stand for 1 hour to remove any bitter juices then rinse and drain thoroughly.

Heat the oil in a large pan. Add the onions and sauté until softened but don't allow them to brown. Stir in the peppers, aubergine, courgettes, garlic and coriander. Cover and simmer for about 40 minutes until everything is just tender but don't let it become mushy.

Stir in the tomatoes and season with salt and pepper. Cover and cook for a further 5 minutes. Add the basil and mix well. Serve warm or cold.

STIR-FRIED FRENCH BEANS

Serves 4

2 tablespoons sesame oil
450 g (1 lb) thin French or
Kenyan beans, topped, tailed
and halved
2 rashers smoked back bacon,
rinded and chopped
4 spring onions, trimmed and
sliced
1 clove of garlic, chopped
100 g (4 oz) mushrooms, wiped
and quartered
50 g (2 oz) canned
waterchestnuts, sliced
1 tablespoon soy sauce
1 tablespoon dry sherry
freshly ground black pepper

Heat the oil in a large heavy-based frying pan or wok. Add the beans and bacon and stir-fry for 2-3 minutes. Stir in the spring onions, garlic and mushrooms and stir-fry for a further 5 minutes.

Add the waterchestnuts, soy sauce, sherry and pepper to taste, blending well. Stir-fry for a further 1 minute. Serve at once.

This is delicious with grilled or toasted meat, especially spare-ribs.

WARM ONION SALAD

Serves 4-6

6 medium onions

DRESSING:
150 ml (¼ pint) walnut oil
3 tablespoons wine vinegar
½ teaspoon Dijon mustard
salt
freshly ground black pepper
1 teaspoon caraway seeds
1 tablespoon chopped fresh
parsley

Place the onions, unpeeled, in a shallow ovenproof dish and bake in a preheated oven, 200°C/400°F (gas mark 6), until tender, about 40-60 minutes. Cool until warm enough to handle then remove the skins and cut into quarters. Separate the onion slices and place in a serving bowl.

To make the dressing, beat the oil with the vinegar, mustard and salt and pepper to taste. Spoon over the still warm onions and toss to coat.

Sprinkle with caraway seeds and parsley and serve warm. This is delicious with cold meats.

ORANGE, BEETROOT AND CHICORY SALAD

Serves 4-6

2 heads of chicory, trimmed
and separated into leaves
3 medium beetroot,
thinly sliced
3 large oranges, peeled, pith
removed and thinly sliced

DRESSING:
4 tablespoons sunflower oil
2 tablespoons cider vinegar
1 teaspoon Dijon mustard
1 teaspoon sugar
small bunch of fresh mint,
finely chopped
salt
freshly ground black pepper

Arrange the chicory, beetroot and oranges in a circular pattern on a large serving dish, slightly overlapping the layers.

To make the dressing, shake the oil with the vinegar, mustard, sugar, mint and salt and pepper to taste in a screw-topped jar.

About 10 minutes before serving, spoon the dressing over the salad.

Warm Onion Salad

Sarah

WARM SPINACH AND BACON SALAD

Serves 4-6

450 g (1 lb) young spinach leaves, trimmed,
washed and dried
6 spring onions, trimmed and finely chopped
1 tablespoon safflower or sunflower oil
1 clove of garlic, peeled and crushed
3 thin rashers bacon, rinded

1 tablespoon sugar
1 tablespoon white wine vinegar
1 tablespoon red wine vinegar
1 egg, beaten
freshly ground black pepper

Tear the spinach leaves into small pieces and place in a serving bowl with the spring onions.

Mash the oil with the garlic and leave to stand while preparing the rest of the salad. Dry-fry the bacon slowly in a frying pan until very crisp. Remove and drain on absorbent paper. Allow the bacon to cool then crumble.

Beat the sugar with the two wine vinegars, egg and pepper to taste. Stir into the warm bacon fat and cook, over a very gentle heat, for a few seconds until lightly thickened.

Add the bacon to the spinach mixture with the strained garlic oil. Pour the warm dressing over the top and toss to coat. Serve immediately.

SOUFLÉED ONION is a delicious and interesting vegetable side dish to serve with roasts and grills. Sauté about 2 medium chopped onions in 40 g (1½ oz) butter until soft but not brown. Sprinkle with 40 g (1½ oz) flour and stir to mix. Gradually add 100 ml (4 fl oz) milk and 100 g (4 oz) grated cheese and stir well. Add 3 beaten egg yolks, mixing well. Remove from the heat and fold in 3 stiffly beaten egg whites with seasoning. Pour into a medium buttered ovenproof dish and bake in a preheated oven, 160°C/325°F (gas mark 3), for 30–40 minutes or until puffed up and lightly browned. Serve at once. Serves 4.

Nanette

GINGERED VEGETABLES

Crisp and full of flavour, this is ideal to serve as part of a Chinese-style meal. It will also go well with plain grilled fish.

Serves 4-6

2 tablespoons sunflower or sesame oil
1 onion, peeled and sliced
2 courgettes, trimmed and sliced
2 carrots, peeled and thinly sliced
1 red or yellow pepper, cored, seeded and thinly sliced
1 green pepper, cored, seeded and thinly sliced

100 g (4 oz) fresh or canned mini corn cobs
small piece of root ginger, peeled and chopped
100 g (4 oz) mangetout, trimmed
1½ teaspoons cornflour
4 tablespoons light soy sauce
2 tablespoons dry sherry
½ teaspoon Chinese 5 spice powder

Heat the oil in a large frying pan or wok. Add the onion, courgettes, carrots, peppers, corn cobs and ginger. Stir-fry for 4 minutes until almost tender but still crisp. Add the mangetout and stir-fry for a further 1 minute.

In a bowl, blend the cornflour with the soy sauce, sherry and Chinese 5 spice powder. Stir into the vegetable mixture and stir-fry for 1-2 minutes until the juices are clear and thickened.

Serve at once.

AFTER-
THOUGHTS

Everyone today is conscious of their diet. We know about additives, cholesterol, vitamins, fibre and calories – and hardly a week goes by when we don't read about some food that is harmful. However, in spite of all that, we still fall prey to temptation every now and again.

Desserts are not a necessity and they are probably not wise, but just occasionally we all throw caution to the wind and enjoy something frivolous.

You don't need a cook book to tell you how to prepare a melon or a peach, to make a fruit salad, or to hull a strawberry. However, when temptation is strong, and you feel the need for something more sinful, one of the following will fit the bill.

Nanette

FRUIT AND NUT CRUNCH

Serves 4

450 g (1 lb) cooking apples,
peeled, cored and cut into
chunks
3 bananas, peeled and sliced
juice of 1 lemon
100 g (4 oz) raspberries, hulled
75 g (3 oz) caster sugar

TOPPING:
225 g (8 oz) soft brown sugar
150 g (5 oz) plain flour
75 g (3 oz) hazelnuts or
walnuts, chopped
50 g (2 oz) muesli
100 g (4 oz) butter

Mix the apples with the bananas, lemon juice, raspberries and sugar. Spoon into a medium ovenproof dish.

To make the topping, mix the sugar with the flour, walnuts and muesli. Melt the butter and add to the dry ingredients, mixing well. Spoon over the fruit mixture.

Bake in a preheated oven, 180°C/350°F (gas mark 4), for 40 minutes, or until golden and bubbly.

Serve hot with vanilla yoghurt or ice cream.

RHUBARB AND STRAWBERRY CRUMBLE

Serves 4 greedy people!

50 g (2 oz) butter
100 g (4 oz) plain wholewheat
flour
50 g (2 oz) brown sugar
pinch of ground nutmeg
450 g (1 lb) rhubarb, chopped
225 g (8 oz) strawberries,
hulled
extra brown sugar (optional)

This is a recipe from a great friend of mine, Angela.

Rub half of the butter into the flour until the mixture resembles fine breadcrumbs. Stir in the sugar and nutmeg. Cook the rhubarb in a little sweetened water until softened. Drain and place in a medium ovenproof dish with the strawberries. Top with the prepared crumble mixture. Sprinkle with some extra brown sugar if you like and dot with the remaining butter.

Bake in a preheated oven, 190°C/375°F (gas mark 5), for 45 minutes. Serve plain or with Proper Custard (see page 140).

TRICIA'S APPLE CRISP

This recipe was given to me by a great friend. It's terribly quick, incredibly good and very easy. It's really an American version of our apple crumble.

Serves 8

6 Granny Smith apples, peeled, cored and very
thinly sliced
juice of 3 lemons
175 g (6 oz) plain flour
2½ teaspoons ground cinnamon

pinch of salt
175 g (6 oz) butter
350 g (12 oz) soft brown sugar
50 g (2 oz) pecans, chopped
50 g (2 oz) walnuts, chopped

Layer the apples in a 20-cm (8-inch) greased round cake tin or 25 x 15-cm (8 x 6-inch) rectangular baking dish, sprinkling lemon juice between each layer. Sift the flour with the cinnamon and salt. Rub in the butter until the mixture resembles fine breadcrumbs. Stir in the sugar and nuts. Spoon evenly over the apple mixture, pressing down firmly.

Bake in a preheated oven, 180°C/350°F (gas mark 4), for 50-60 minutes, or until the apples are cooked and the topping is crisp and golden brown.

Serve hot with ice cream.

This works just as well with blueberries, only leave out the cinnamon.

Sarah

Nanette

PATRIOTIC PUDDING

This was served at a friend's home in America before watching an English football match. Why it's patriotic I don't know. We certainly were. Sadly England lost, but the recipe is a winner.

Serves 6

100 g (4 oz) butter	1½ teaspoons baking powder
100 g (4 oz) caster sugar	3 very ripe bananas, peeled and mashed
2 eggs, beaten	2 tablespoons brown rum
175 g (6 oz) plain flour	grated rind of 1 orange

Cream the butter with the sugar until pale and fluffy. Add the eggs, a little at a time, with 1 tablespoon of the flour. Sift the remaining flour with the baking powder and fold into the creamed mixture. Stir in the bananas, rum and orange rind.

Spoon into a well-buttered 1.2 litre (2-pint) pudding basin. Cover with a circle of buttered greaseproof paper and a piece of greased foil which has been pleated to allow for expansion. Secure with string. Place in a steamer or on a trivet in a saucepan half-full of water and steam, over a moderate heat, for 1 ¾ hours.

To serve, invert the pudding onto a warmed serving dish. Serve with crème fraîche and slices of banana, if liked, or with Proper Custard (see page 140).

If you ever need to conjure up a quick dessert, make a ZABAGLIONE. Place 4 egg yolks and 2 tablespoons caster sugar in the top of a double boiler (or a bowl set over a pan of simmering water). Beat well then add ½ glass of Marsala wine (or other sweet white wine) and keep beating until pale and very thick. Serve immediately with ratafia biscuits. Serves 4

Nanette

UPSIDE-DOWN PEACH PUDDING

This is a real nursery pudding, elevated to grown-up status by serving it with a special really creamy sauce.

Serves 6

TOPPING:
50 g (2 oz) butter
100 g (4 oz) soft dark brown sugar
4 firm peaches, peeled and stoned

BASE:
100 g (4 oz) plain flour
½ teaspoon bicarbonate of soda
1 teaspoon ground ginger
pinch of ground nutmeg
pinch of ground cloves
pinch of salt

2 teaspoons ground cinnamon
1 egg, beaten
100 g (4 oz) brown sugar
75 g (3 oz) black treacle
100 ml (4 fl oz) milk
2 teaspoons lemon juice
50 g (2 oz) butter or margarine, melted

SAUCE:
150 ml (¼ pint) double cream, whipped
150 ml (¼ pint) natural yoghurt
1 tablespoon caster sugar

To make the topping, melt the butter in a pan. Add the sugar and cook for 2 minutes. Pour into a 20-cm (8-inch) round cake tin. Slice each peach into quarters. Arrange the peaches over the topping in an attractive pattern.

To make the base, sift the flour with the bicarbonate of soda, ginger, nutmeg, cloves, salt and cinnamon. Beat the egg with the sugar, treacle, milk and lemon juice. Stir into the flour mixture with the butter or margarine and mix well. Spoon evenly over the peaches to cover. Bake in a preheated oven, 190°C/375°F (gas mark 5), for 50-70 minutes, or until well risen, golden brown and cooked.

SCHOOL PUDDING

I am one of the very few people who actually loved school food. So much so that I was really put out during one period of my school life when my mother went on a great health kick – I was given packed lunches that consisted of wholewheat bread and things like alfalfa, sprouted mung beans and yeast extract. I used to look so longingly at the school toad-in-the-hole, spotted dick and roly-poly pudding with lumpy custard that in the end my Mother succumbed. Although I now (in the perverse way children have) eat healthy food from choice, once a year I indulge my nostalgia with this School Pudding and some custard.

Serves 6

100 g (4 oz) fresh breadcrumbs
100 g (4 oz) shredded suet
25 g (1 oz) plain flour
75 g (3 oz) sugar
75 g (3 oz) apricot jam

75 g (3 oz) sultanas
juice of 1 lemon
grated rind of 2 lemons
3 eggs, beaten

Mix the breadcrumbs with the suet, flour, sugar, jam, sultanas, lemon juice and rind. Add the eggs, beating well to make a smooth mixture. Spoon into a well-buttered 1.2-litre (2-pint) pudding basin. Cover with a circle of buttered greaseproof paper and a piece of greased foil pleated to allow for expansion. Secure with string. Place in a steamer or on a trivet in a saucepan half-full of water and steam, over a moderate heat, for 1 hour.

To serve, invert the pudding onto a warmed serving dish. Serve with Proper Custard (see page 140) or ice cream.

HIP-HUGGING PUDDING

Serves 8-10

25 g (1 oz) plain flour
75 g (3 oz) sultanas
50 g (2 oz) ground almonds
½ teaspoon ground cloves
½ teaspoon ground cinnamon
50 g (2 oz) walnuts, chopped
1 small apple, peeled and grated
100 g (4 oz) sugar
6 eggs, separated

For those men who get misty-eyed about syrup pudding, or spotted dick, and all those other desserts reminiscent of school lunches, here is a pudding that will gladden their hearts.

Mix the flour with the sultanas, ground almonds, cloves, cinnamon, walnuts, apple and sugar. Add the egg yolks, one at a time, mixing well. Whisk the egg whites until they stand in stiff peaks. Fold into the mixture. Spoon into a buttered 1.8-litre (3-pint) ring mould or baking tin. Bake in a preheated oven, 180°C/350°F (gas mark 4), for 40-50 minutes, until well risen, golden and cooked.

Serve hot with Proper Custard (see below).

PROPER CUSTARD

Serves 4-6

2 large egg yolks
300 ml (½ pint) milk
1 tablespoon sugar
1 vanilla pod

Beat the egg yolks in a bowl. Heat the milk with the sugar and vanilla pod until almost boiling. Remove the vanilla pod and pour the milk over the egg yolks, mixing well. Return to the pan and cook, over a low heat, until the custard thickens slightly (or will thinly coat the back of a spoon), stirring frequently.

Serve warm or cold.

A lot of people love rice pudding. Cook some rice in the usual way and drain. When cold, fold it into thick cream or crème fraîche. Spoon into glasses. Purée some prunes and put a spoonful on top.

Nanette

SWEET PASTRY

Makes enough to line a
23-cm (9-inch) flan or tart

225 g (8 oz) plain flour
pinch of salt
150 g (5 oz) butter
2 teaspoons icing sugar
1 egg yolk
few drops of iced water

This is the recipe I use for sweet flans and tarts.

Put the flour, salt, butter, icing sugar and egg yolk in a food processor and process until the mixture is crumbly, about ½ minute. Add a few drops of water, with the motor running, and process until the mixture forms a dough ball. Wrap in clingfilm and chill for 30 minutes before using.

Alternatively, sift the flour with the salt into a bowl. Rub in the butter until the mixture resembles fine breadcrumbs. Stir in the sugar, egg yolk and a few drops of water and bind to a smooth dough. Knead lightly and chill as before.

I always roll out this pastry between two sheets of greaseproof paper — it stops it from sticking but you can roll it out in the usual way if you wish.   *Nanette*

PECAN PIE

Serves 8

1 quantity Sweet Pastry (see
above)
5 eggs
50 g (2 oz) muscovado sugar
1 teaspoon vanilla essence
25 g (1 oz) butter, melted
475 ml (16 fl oz) maple syrup
25 g (1 oz) plain flour
grated rind of 1 lemon
100 g (4 oz) pecan halves

Pecan Pie is as American as Apple Pie is English – only better.

Roll out the pastry and use to line a 23-cm (9-inch) pie plate or flan dish. Beat the eggs with the sugar and vanilla essence until thick and glossy. Stir in the butter, maple syrup and flour, mixing well. Pour into the pastry case and sprinkle with the lemon rind. Top with the pecan halves – don't worry if they appear to float.

Bake in a preheated oven, 180°C/350°F (gas mark 4), for about 50 minutes, or until the filling has set and the pastry is cooked. Allow to cool then chill thoroughly.

Serve this very sweet pie with chilled whipped cream or vanilla ice cream.

Emma

ALMOND AND PEAR FLAN

If you can't get fresh pears then use canned.

Serves 6-8

BASE:
225 g (8 oz) digestive biscuits, crushed
75 g (3 oz) butter, melted

FILLING:
100 g (4 oz) butter
100 g (4 oz) caster sugar
3 eggs

100 g (4 oz) self-raising flour
100 g (4 oz) ground almonds
1½ tablespoons milk
½ teaspoon vanilla essence
2 large Comice pears, peeled, cored and quartered
caster or vanilla sugar to sprinkle
25 g (1 oz) flaked almonds, toasted (optional)

To make the base, mix the digestive biscuit crumbs with the butter. Press into a 30-cm (12-inch) ovenproof flan tin or dish and chill.

To make the filling, beat the butter with the sugar until pale and creamy. Beat in the eggs, one at a time, mixing well. Fold in the flour with the almonds, milk and vanilla essence. Plunge the pears into a bowl of boiling water, leave for ½ minute then remove.

Spoon the creamed mixture over the flan base – don't worry if there does not seem to be a great deal of mixture, it does rise during cooking. Arrange the pears on top in an attractive circular pattern, pressing into the mixture. Sprinkle with a little caster or vanilla sugar. Bake in a preheated oven, 200°C/400°F (gas mark 6), for 20-25 minutes.

Serve warm, sprinkled with the toasted almonds if liked.

To make vanilla sugar, all you need to do is leave a vanilla pod in your caster sugar, overnight.

Almond and Pear Flan

BLACK CHERRY TART

On a trip to Italy in June, we drove north from Rome to the region of Umbria, past fields of wheat and oats, castles perched on hilltops and vast stretches of sunflowers turning their yellow heads to face the sun. We arrived at Fernando's house in the afternoon and had this Black Cherry Tart, made locally in the village, for tea. Whenever I make it, the memories flood back of that afternoon sitting on a sun-drenched terrace – knowing it was raining in England.

Serves 6-8

PASTRY:
200 g (7 oz) plain flour
90 g (3½ oz) butter
25 g (1 oz) caster sugar
3 tablespoons cold water

FILLING:
700 g (1½ lb) black cherries, stoned
75 g (3 oz) plain flour
100 g (4 oz) sugar
4 eggs
300 ml (½ pint) single cream

To make the pastry, sift the flour into a bowl. Rub in the butter until the mixture resembles fine breadcrumbs. Stir in the sugar. Add sufficient water to bind to a dough. Knead lightly, wrap in clingfilm and chill for 30 minutes or until required.

Roll out the pastry and use to line a rectangular, loose-bottomed, shallow baking tin, measuring about 25 x 25 cm (10 x 6 inches). Prick and bake 'blind' in a preheated oven, 190°C/375°F (gas mark 5), for 10 minutes to par-bake. Remove from the oven and fill with the cherries.

Beat the flour with the sugar and eggs. Gradually add the cream, beating well. Pour the mixture over the cherries. Reduce the oven temperature to 180°C/350°F (gas mark 4). Bake the tart for 30-35 minutes until the pastry is crisp and golden and the filling is cooked.

Serve just warm.

TART LEMON TART: Line a 23-cm (9-inch) tin with ready-bought shortcrust pastry. Bake blind for 20 minutes in a preheated oven, 190°C/375°F (gas mark 5). Beat together 2 eggs and 50 g (2 oz) caster sugar. When thick, add juice and grated rind of 2 lemons, 100 g (4 oz) of melted butter and 100 g (4 oz) ground almonds. Pour this into the pastry case and bake until set (about 25 minutes). Serve well chilled.

Nanette

CAMILLA'S TART

Serves 4-6

PASTRY:	FILLING:
175 g (6 oz) plain flour	225 g (8 oz) cream cheese
pinch of salt	175 g (6 oz) sugar
75 g (3 oz) butter	150 ml (¼ pint) double cream
1 egg, beaten	3 eggs, beaten
	50 g (2 oz) sultanas

To make the pastry, sift the flour and the salt into a bowl. Rub in the butter until the mixture resembles fine breadcrumbs. Stir in the egg and a little water if necessary to mix to a firm but pliable dough. Knead lightly until smooth. Roll out on a lightly floured surface to a round large enough to line a 23-cm (9-inch) greased, loose-bottomed, fluted flan tin. Bake 'blind' in a preheated oven,

190°C/375°F (gas mark 5), for 10-15 minutes, to par-bake.

Meanwhile, beat the cheese with the sugar until creamy. Add the cream, eggs and sultanas, mixing well. Pour into the part-baked flan case, return to the oven and bake for a further 25-30 minutes, until cooked and firm.

Eat plain or serve just warm topped with fresh raspberries or blueberries.

BLACKBERRY TART makes a super late summer dessert. Chop 150 g (5 oz) walnuts in a food processor. Add 175 g (6 oz) plain flour and 100 g (4 oz) butter and process briefly. Add 60 g (2½ oz) sugar and 1 egg and process until the mixture holds together. Chill for about 20 minutes then press into a 23-cm (9-inch) flan tin or dish. Bake in a preheated oven, 180°C/350°F (gas mark 4), for 20 minutes and cool. When cool, pile about 450 g (1 lb) hulled blackberries into the tart crust. Melt 175 g (6 oz) jar of blackcurrant jelly over a low heat. Sprinkle 1 dessertspoon powdered gelatine over 3 tablespoons orange juice and leave to soften. Stir into the blackcurrant jelly then leave until nearly cool and syrupy. Brush over the blackberries to glaze. Chill and serve with Greek-style yoghurt. Serves 6.

Emma

RHUBARB CHEESECAKE

Serves 4-6

BASE:
225 g (8 oz) ginger biscuits, crushed
25 g (1 oz) Demerara sugar
75 g (3 oz) butter, melted

FILLING:
450 g (1 lb) rhubarb, trimmed and cut into
even-sized pieces
175 g (6 oz) caster sugar
100 ml (4 fl oz) water
piece of pared orange rind
450 g (1 lb) cream cheese
2 eggs, beaten
150 ml (¼ pint) double cream

To make the base, mix the biscuit crumbs with the sugar. Add the butter and stir to coat. Use to line the base of a 20-cm (8-inch) greased, loose-bottomed cake tin. Chill thoroughly.

To make the filling, place the rhubarb, half of the sugar and water in a heavy-based pan. Add the orange rind and cook gently until the rhubarb is tender. Allow to cool then remove and discard the orange rind. Beat the cream cheese with the eggs, remaining sugar and cream until thick.

Add three-quarters of the cooked rhubarb and swirl to mix. Pour over the prepared biscuit base and bake in a preheated oven, 160°C/325°F (gas mark 3), for 30-40 minutes, until firm and set. Remove from the oven and allow to cool completely in the tin.

To serve, carefully unmould the cooked cheesecake from the tin and place on a serving plate. Top with the remaining rhubarb and chill thoroughly.

Serve cut into thick wedges.

I like to make this cheesecake with uncooked raspberries.

Sarah

CHOCOLATE PIE

Serves 4-6

BASE:
50 g (2 oz) butter
50 g (2 oz) sugar
350 g (12 oz) rolled oats
40 g (1½ oz) plain flour

FILLING:
450 g (1 lb) cream cheese

175 g (6 oz) caster sugar
2 eggs, beaten
100 g (4 oz) plain chocolate, melted
2 teaspoons coffee powder
1 tablespoon hot water
150 ml (¼ pint) soured cream
1 teaspoon vanilla essence
grated chocolate

To make the base, cream the butter with the sugar until light and fluffy. Stir in the oats and flour. Press the mixture onto the base of a lightly greased 23-cm (9-inch) loose-bottomed cake tin. Bake in a preheated oven, 200°C/400°F (gas mark 6), for 15 minutes.

To make the filling, cream the cheese with the sugar until light and fluffy. Gradually add the eggs, mixing well. Fold in the chocolate, coffee dissolved in the water, soured cream and vanilla essence. Pour onto the cooked base.

Reduce the oven temperature to 160°C/325°F (gas mark 3), and bake the pie for a further 40 minutes, or until firm to the touch. Remove from the oven and allow to cool.

When cool sprinkle with finely grated chocolate.

I brought both my daughters up on 'healthy' food — wholemeal bread, vegetables and fruit being the mainstay of their diet, and hardly any sweets or chocolate. I say this is why they have beautiful skins and great teeth. They say it's why they now go on chocolate binges, because they were deprived. Ah, well! you just can't win.

Nanette

OREO COOKIE CHEESECAKE

If you're not married and want to be, making this cheesecake is a sure way of getting a marriage proposal fast, provided your boyfriend is thin.

Serves 12-14

BASE:
350 g (12 oz) oreo cookies (oreo cookies, although expensive, are to be found in England but if you can't get them use chocolate bourbon biscuits instead), crushed
100 g (4 oz) butter, melted

FILLING:
800 g (1¼ lb) cream cheese
4 eggs, beaten

175 g (6 oz) caster sugar
200 ml (7 fl oz) single cream
350 g (12 oz) oreo cookies or chocolate bourbon biscuits, coarsely broken into small pieces
400 g (14 oz) soured cream
2 tablespoons caster sugar

TOPPING:
4 tablespoons soured cream
chocolate curls

To make the base, mix the crushed cookies or biscuits with the butter. Press firmly into a 30- to 35-cm (12-14-inch) diameter spring-form cake tin.

To make the filling, beat the cream cheese with the eggs and caster sugar until smooth. Stir in the single cream and pour half of this filling over the base. Top with the broken biscuits and press into the filling. Cover with the remaining cream cheese mixture.

Place on a baking sheet, and bake in a preheated oven, 190°C/375°F (gas mark 5), for 25 minutes, or until the cheesecake

is fairly set around the edges of the tin.

Remove from the oven and increase the oven temperature to 240°C/475°F (gas mark 9).

Mix the soured cream with the sugar and spread over the top of the cheesecake. When the oven reaches the new temperature, return to the oven and bake for exactly 5 minutes. Remove from the oven and allow to cool thoroughly.

For the topping, spread the remaining 4 tablespoons of soured cream over the cheesecake and sprinkle with the chocolate curls.

Oreo Cookie Cheesecake

Nanette

LYN'S COFFEE CHOCOLATE SOUFFLÉS

Makes 4-5

100 ml (4 fl oz) single cream
2 heaped teaspoons of instant coffee
100 g (4 oz) best cooking chocolate
2 tablespoons brandy
3 eggs, separated
2 tablespoons caster sugar

Prepare 4 small ovenproof ramekin dishes by buttering lightly then coating with a little caster sugar.

Combine the cream, coffee and chocolate in a double saucepan or a bowl over a pan of simmering water, whisking lightly until dissolved and blended. Remove from heat. Whisk in the brandy, and the egg yolks, one at a time.

In a separate bowl, beat the egg whites until frothy, then continue beating while you slowly add the sugar, until the mixture forms stiff peaks. Fold the two mixtures together carefully. Pour into the soufflé dishes. Place in a preheated oven, 200°C/400°F (gas mark 6), for 12 minutes, or put in the refrigerator while you have your main course, then pop in oven, while you clear the dishes. You can serve with cream if you wish.

The friend who gave me the recipe said that the mixture will stretch to five soufflés quite easily.

Emma

YOGHURT BRULÉE

Serves 6

150 ml (¼ pint) double cream
450 g (1 lb) Greek-style yoghurt
2 eggs yolks, beaten
1 tablespoon clear honey
¼ teaspoon vanilla essence
75 g (3 oz) dark brown sugar

This is my own version of my favourite pudding – crème brulée.

Mix the cream with the yoghurt, egg yolks, honey and vanilla essence in the top of a double boiler or in a bowl over a pan of simmering water. Cook gently for about 5 minutes, stirring constantly, until the mixture will coat the back of a spoon.

Pour into six small ramekin dishes and sprinkle evenly with the sugar. Caramelise under a preheated hot grill until golden and bubbly. Allow to cool, then chill thoroughly to serve for about 4-6 hours.

CHOCOLATE MINT MOUSSE

Serves 8

3 eggs, separated
175 g (6 oz) caster sugar
3 tablespoons crème de menthe
2 teaspoons coffee powder
400 g (14 oz) plain chocolate
75 g (3 oz) butter
450 ml (¾ pint) double cream

Beat the egg yolks with the sugar until thick and creamy. Add the crème de menthe and coffee dissolved in a little hot water, mixing well.

Break the chocolate into a bowl, add the butter and melt over a pan of hot water. Add the egg yolk mixture, mixing well. Whip the cream until it stands in soft peaks and fold into the chocolate mixture.

Whisk the egg whites until they stand in stiff peaks and fold into the chocolate mixture. Pour into a 900-ml (1½-pint) serving dish or eight small wine glasses and chill to set. Serve chilled.

EXTRA RICH CHOCOLATE MOUSSE

Serves 4

225 g (8 oz) plain chocolate
2 tablespoons liqueur (for example, brandy, rum or Tia Maria)
4 eggs, separated
whipped cream
crumbled chocolate flake bar to decorate

Break the chocolate into pieces and melt in the top of a double boiler or in a bowl over a pan of simmering water. Add the chosen liqueur and stir quickly to mix. Beat in the egg yolks, one at a time, then remove from the heat.

Whisk the egg whites until they stand in stiff peaks. Fold into the chocolate mixture. Pour into one dish or four small ramekin dishes and chill to set.

Serve topped with a little whipped cream and sprinkled with crumbled chocolate flake bar to decorate.

FOOLED MANGO is the perfect light dessert to serve after a hearty main course. Purée the flesh of 2 very ripe mangoes with the juice of 1 lime and 1 heaped tablespoon of clear honey. Whip the cream until thick and fold into the mango purée. Serve chilled in tall wine glasses. Serves 4.

Emma

PLUMS IN GRAND MARNIER

Serves 4

75 g (3 oz) caster sugar
300 ml (½ pint) water
450 (1 lb) red plums, left
whole
grated rind of 1 orange
3 tablespoons Grand Marnier

Place the sugar and water in a heavy-based pan and heat gently until the sugar dissolves. Add the plums and orange rind and simmer gently until the plums are cooked, about 10-15 minutes. Stir in the Grand Marnier and transfer to a serving bowl.

Serve warm or cold with whipped cream.

BAKED BANANAS WITH HONEY AND ALMONDS

Serves 4

4 bananas, peeled
4 tablespoons clear or set
honey
50 g (2 oz) flaked almonds
4 teaspoons brown sugar
2 tablespoons brown rum

This is a really quick, last-minute dessert, which is a great emergency standby.

Slice each banana in half lengthways. Place in a shallow ovenproof dish. Drizzle over the honey and sprinkle with the almonds and sugar. Spoon over the rum, cover and bake in a preheated oven, 200°C/400°F (gas mark 6), for about 10-12 minutes until just tender and bubbly.

Serve warm with whipped cream.

Everyone knows I have basket-mania. I use baskets for everything — fruit, flowers, make-up, magazines, etc. I have a collection of very small baskets, found on a trip to France, that I use when strawberries are at their very best. I like to serve each guest with their own basket of strawberries, sitting in the middle of a large plate, with a small mound of thick cream on the side. Guests then help themselves to lemon or orange quarters to squeeze over, sugar or ground pepper.

Nanette

SARAH'S RASPBERRY SOUFFLÉ

Makes 6-8

275 g (10 oz) chilled
raspberries
4 egg whites
100 g (4 oz) caster sugar
150 ml (6 fl oz) cream or
crème fraîche

Pulverise the raspberries. In a separate bowl, beat the egg whites until frothy, then add the caster sugar, slowly beating until stiff (but not dry). Fold in the raspberry purée.

Prepare 6-8 (depending on size) ramekin dishes by buttering lightly then coating with a little caster sugar. Divide the mixture between the ramekin dishes and bake at 190°C/375°F (gas mark 5), for about 12 minutes until the soufflés have puffed up.

Serve with the cream or crème fraîche.

For really special occasions, you could try stirring 2 tablespoons of framboise liqueur into the cream.

RITZ DESSERT

Serves 4-6

3 egg whites
225 g (8 oz) caster sugar
½ teaspoon baking powder
14 Ritz crackers, crushed
75 g (3 oz) hazlenuts, chopped
300 ml (½ pint) double cream

When I first had this at my friend Barbara's house I thought it was delicious but had no idea what it was.

Whisk the egg whites until frothy. Add the sugar a tablespoon at a time, and baking powder, whisking constantly, until very stiff. Fold in the crackers and nuts. Spoon into a greased 23-cm/9-inch pie tin or ovenproof flan dish and level the surface. Bake in a preheated oven, 160°C/325°F (gas mark 3), for 35 minutes. Remove from the oven and allow to cool then chill thoroughly, about 24 hours.

Whip the cream until it stands in soft peaks. Pile or pipe on top of the dessert to serve.

REDCURRANTS WITH MELON

Serves 4

450 g (1 lb) redcurrants,
topped and tailed
3 tablespoons sugar
1 Charentais melon
icing sugar to decorate

Place three-quarters of the redcurrants and sugar in a small pan and cook, over a very low heat, until the sugar has dissolved and the juices run from the fruit. Whirl in a blender or food processor, strain through a sieve and chill.

Peel the melon, remove the seeds and cut lengthways into very thin slices. Arrange on a large plate in a decorative fan shape.

Carefully spoon the chilled redcurrant sauce over the melon and decorate with the remaining berries. Serve sprinkled with icing sugar.

MELON SORBET

Serves 4-6

700 g (1½ lb) melon flesh
275 g (10 oz) caster sugar
300 ml (½ pint) boiling water

Purée the melon in a blender or food processor until smooth. Mix the sugar with the boiling water and stir to dissolve. Mix with the melon purée, measure and make up to 1.2 litres (2 pints) with cold water if necessary. Pour into a freezer tray and freeze for 30 minutes or until mushy.

Remove from the freezer and whisk well to break down any ice crystals. Return to the freezer tray and freeze again for a further 30 minutes. Repeat then freeze until firm.

Remove the sorbet from the freezer about 10 minutes before required to soften slightly.

Serve scooped into chilled glasses.

This is nice served in small melon shells.

Redcurrants with Melon

BROWN BREAD ICE CREAM

Serves 4-6

75 g (3 oz) brown breadcrumbs
50 g (2 oz) Demerara sugar
4 eggs, separated
300 ml (½ pint) double cream
50 g (2 oz) caster sugar

Mix the breadcrumbs and Demerara sugar together and bake in a pre-heated, medium oven until pale and crunchy (not burnt!). Cool. Lightly beat the egg yolks. Whisk the double cream until thick. Whisk the egg whites until stiff and then fold in the caster sugar. Fold all the ingredients together and freeze in a suitable container. Serve scooped into wine glasses.

GREEN GUNPOWDER TEA ICE CREAM

Serves 4-6

150 ml (¼ pint) freshly made
strong green gunpowder tea
juice of ½ lemon
4 egg yolks
100 g (4 oz) caster sugar
600 ml (1 pint) double cream

Mix the cold tea with the lemon juice. Beat the egg yolks with the sugar until thick and creamy. Heat the cream until very hot but do not allow to boil. Beat into the egg mixture, blending well. Add the tea and stir, over a very gentle heat, until the mixture begins to thicken and will coat the back of a spoon. Allow to cool then pour into a freezer tray. Freeze until mushy, about 1-2 hours.

Remove from the freezer and whisk to break down any large egg crystals. Return to the freezer tray and freeze until firm.

Remove the ice cream from the freezer about 20 minutes before required to soften slightly. Serve scooped into chilled wine glasses.

INDEX

Acknowledgements

All three of us would like to give an enormous thank you to Becky, Barbara and Graeme for all their hard work.

We would also like to thank Henry Green, Ros Sacher and Heidi O'Grady of Jerry's Home Stores for helping us with the props for the food photography, Geoffrey Libson of Chattelmania for the props used in the cover photograph and Annabel Hobbs of Michaeljohn.

MICHAELJOHN
25 Albemarle Street
London
W1X 4LH

JERRY'S HOME STORE
163-167 Fulham Road
London
SW3 6SN

CHATTELMANIA
186-188 Kentish Town Road
London
NW5 2AE